P9-CCA-377

Written by
mba mbulu
Copyright © 1995 All Rights Reserved
No unauthorized duplication permitted
A Production of
"The People"
P.O. Box 50334
Washington, D. C. 20091-0334

ISBN 1-883885-10-8

Made in the U. S. of A.

...not to be
is the exclusive property of
mba mbulu,
who retains all rights to its ownership and exploitation
Copyright © 1995 All Rights Reserved
No unauthorized duplication permitted
A Production of
"The People"
P.O. Box 50334
Washington, D. C. 20091-0334

ISBN 1-883885-10-8
LCIP Pending

We Publish Honest Black Writings. We Are
"The People"

TABLE OF CONTENTS

...not to be

A brief comment on the defrauding of white America by America's white leadership, and how white Americans are handicapped as a result.

CONTENTS

So it came to pass, not being.

First there were the American people. Then there was the American government. And then there were American commercial interests.

Now there are American commercial interests. Then there are American leaders. And then there are the American people.

When the American people are able to accept the extent to which they have been betrayed by their government and leaders, it is possible that they will be again.

But the American people are not yet able.

From the very beginning, and at every turn, America's leaders have tricked the American people. From the very beginning and at every turn America's leaders have sold out on the interests of America's people in favor of maximizing the profits of America's commercial interests, even to the point of undermining the people's educational aspirations. The school system is supposed to educate Americans so that they develop their individual potential to function as healthy members of society. Instead, it has been manipulated to the end of developing individual skills and talents that can be used by the commercial community to advance its commercial interests. That explains why Americans are the most schooled but least educated people one is apt to encounter.

The further a person goes through America's schooling process, the less common sense he/she seems to possess. Common sense is what an educational process is supposed to build on. Strangely, America's educational process scorns common sense (it is not good that workers think independently; the production process might suffer) and, in so doing, stagnates the development of America's individuals.

Not To Be 7

If Americans were properly educated, the first principle they would be made to understand is that people have at least two natural enemies— bad government and big business— and that commercial interests always seduce and corrupt government leaders in order to legally "screw" the people. This reality recurs so frequently not because it is an uncontrollable or unpredictable part of the socio-government process, but because America's leaders and America's business community deliberately conspire against the American people. When the American people are able to accept this fact, that they are deliberately screwed by their leaders, that their leaders consciously and consistently conspire against them (in much the same manner that they conspire against Black People and other "minorities"), then they can begin to retake control of their government. But the American people are not yet able.

Because their leaders and business interests have conspired so successfully against them, the American people have a warped understanding of the human family, women, races and race relations, economics, the socialization process, sports, the environment and a host of other critical studies that must be understood and fused appropriately if human beings are to experience life to its fullest. Because the American people have been systematically weaned of much of their common sense, they don't realize that their train of thought is warped. Like any socially underdeveloped people, they think that everybody who opposes or criticizes them is "out to get them." In this particular case, it is the equivalent of the knot calling the rest of the tire bad.

It cannot be denied. The American people, white people, have been led to a state of disconnectedness with most of the rest of the world's peoples. They have been

NOT TO BE

deceived and misused and underdeveloped by political leaders and business interests. But the American people cannot expect to get away without taking some of the blame for their condition. Certainly, they were overwhelmed by the intoxicating mythology of white superiority, by the rituals of white supremacy that were professed everywhere and unchallenged by anyone who counted. Certainly, from the day he or she was born the American individual was primed to be a spoke in the hub of an American business. Certainly, they did not realize that they meant little more to their leaders and business interests than any other work force (including slaves), but many of them knew that they were being made party to a major human travesty, a huge untruth. They acquiesced anyway; because everybody else was acquiescing, because there was no powerful force instructing them otherwise, and because they <u>wanted</u> to believe they are superior to other people. They wanted to turn their noses up at someone else, to pad their ego at the expense of some less fortunate person, and to compensate for their own lack of self-worth. Their leaders and business interests have taken advantage of that despicable desire and made big time suckers out of them.

Who in the world would grasp onto such a dehumanizing concept as "poor white trash?" Who else, but American white people. Unfortunately, the concept is a valid one; there is a great deal of poor white trash in America. But, contrary to popular opinion, that poor white trash is not in the hills of Tennessee, the dirt towns of the South or at the bottom of white America's social pyramid. No, America's poor white trash is at the top of the pyramid; composed of state and federal legislators and congressmen, presidents, chairpersons and major stockholders of America's most influential businesses, controllers of America's media, members of America's most acclaimed "societies," socialites, et cetera. In short, America's poor white trash is in control of this country. They are poor because they are spiritually bankrupt; they don't have any values that the prospect of profit can't nullify. And, they are trash because they are knowingly ruining the very fiber of decency with their preference for low-level morals, their lack of humanity, their love of "the Almighty dollar" and their arrogant belief that they have a right to live at the expense of somebody else's blood, sweat and tears. Poor white trash thrives in America, and it will continue to run this country into the ground until the average white citizen is able to draw a halt to all of this white insanity. But the average white citizen is not quite able to do this yet.

The American people, white people, have been suckered to the point where they are not able to take the steps they need to take in order to free themselves from the mental domination of their "elites." Some of them are trying to rewrite history, to make it more real, objective and truthful, but the new histories they are producing are stillborn in the eyes of non-white peoples. The radical writings of America's new liberals and multiculturalists is outdated before it is even printed because it refuses to accept the progressive primacy of non-white peoples as a starting point. These well-meaning but disabled whites who are breaking with the white establishment cannot accept the primacy of Black human development. They are unable to even consider the proposition that Black People were more knowledgeable, sophisticated and socially advanced 5000 years ago than white people are today. It is impossible for them to think that there were Black People 5000 years ago who could have accessed much of today's

NOT TO BE

technology, but refused to do so because they realized that the long range consequences would be more devastating than beneficial. Today's white newthinkers can't think such thoughts because, in spite of the conscious break with the white establishment, they can't break with their subconscious certainty that white people know more, are smarter and are better equipped to lead and monitor mankind than non-white peoples.

So non-white peoples will go on without white people, and in spite of white people.

A new world stage has been set. Its major players, though already known, are yet to take their places. The American people in particular, and white people in general, have indicated that they are unwilling to take part in this new order. They somehow seem to think that they have more to lose, more of value to protect, than everybody else. Such thoughts indicate, first of all, that they are not developed enough to be granted a major role on this new stage. Rather than bolster its quality, they would reduce it and represent decay, a bad apple in the midst of an otherwise healthy barrel. Secondly, these thoughts indicate that the American people have been suckered to the point where they are unable to effectively distinguish between reality and propaganda. The propaganda, the white mythology line, still insists that the play cannot go on without whites. The reality is the exact opposite!

As soon as people begin contemplating and discussing the future, the future becomes more a function and property of today than tomorrow. Non-white people are welcoming the future with open arms and commitment, while the American people and white people in general are acting as if it has not arrived. By the time they acknowledge its presence, white people will be too far behind to do anything but follow.

Perhaps, it is better that way.

The American people are not yet able. They are not yet able because they have been brainwashed and miseducated so thoroughly that they can not acknowledge the fact of their victimization. As participants, as actors, as players, American individuals can not effectively distinguish between the imagery of whiteness and the reality of a new world order. People of color have forged ahead, the white elite is unwilling to adjust for economic reasons, and the American people, who would benefit from the change, don't know how to adapt on their own.

When all else fails, each of us has the responsibility of raising and developing him/her self. Nature provides each of us with the basic qualities we need to be good. Each person has the responsibility of selecting the proper models and adjusting accordingly. The models are plentiful, if the desire to be is strong enough. Not so in the United States of America. The people here, white people, are not yet able.

the

hispanic

factor

A look at the possibility of African-Americans and Hispanic Americans forming a political bloc as a means of combatting white America's racism.

CONTENTS

[NOTE: The term "hispanic" is used here because of its convenience, not its accuracy. For the author, "hispanic" is a pejorative term; it suggests a person who is somewhat less than a pure Spaniard. Spanish speaking people of South and Central America and the Caribbean prefer to be identified by their country, and the pejorative connotations that the term "hispanic" carries partly explains this preference.]

Because there are so many Hispanic persons being settled in the midst of Black People in the United States of America, because some of them compete with African-Americans for low level employment opportunities and other services and benefits, and because others are assimilated by the white status quo and take on the attitude warps of the white status quo, the question of African-American and Hispanic political unity has become a frequently mentioned one. When considering this question, all of Us must keep two facts in mind:

(1) Hispanic society is a racist society. Therefore, most of the Hispanics who come to this country come as racists, bringing their racist ideas, prejudices, expectations and inclinations with them; and

(2) There is no tension between African-Americans and African-Hispanics who come to this country that is not typical of the tensions that exist in the Black Community in general. African-Americans do not experience any racist drifts when African-Hispanics settle in Our midst, therefore We have no reason to react negatively to this mixture. If African-Americans react negatively when white and/or mixed Hispanics enter Black areas, it is because these Hispanics have deliberately or unknowingly projected an attitude that is offensive to Black People.

The Hispanic Factor   15

It is necessary to briefly expound on the first point before moving on.

Hispanic society is a racist society, and the Hispanics who come to this country bring their racist propensities with them. First of all, 97% to 98% of the Hispanics who legally enter this country are non-Black [This does not apply to Puerto Rican Hispanics, since Puerto Rico is all but an American state]. Every informed American knows that the United States government has an immigration policy that discriminates against Black immigrants, but that can only partly explain the fact that such a small number of Black Hispanic immigrants are coming to this country at a time when Hispanic immigration is being encouraged. Are we to believe that only white Hispanics are applying to Hispanic governments for permission to immigrate to the United States, or is it that Blacks who want to leave Hispanic countries are not allowed to do so as liberally as white Hispanics? Having lived in the midst of racist people and racist institutions all of my life, I can imagine that the Brothers and Sisters in Hispanic countries must be facing obstacles that non-Black Hispanics do not have to overcome. Directly and indirectly, Hispanic governments must be exercising an immigration policy in a manner that discriminates against their Black citizens.

But that is not surprising in the least. Racism is part of the white Hispanic pulse, just as it is part of white America's pulse. Spain, the "mother country" that colonized the Hispanic areas, is a white European country built on racism, violence and bigotry, just like England, France, Germany, Russia and the rest. Spanish prejudices and inclinations were passed on to the Hispanic classes, and it follows Hispanics wherever they go. If one wants to see it jump out at you, simply look at the Hispanic communications media.

16   **NOT TO BE**

In the United States, there are two national Hispanic television networks, Univision and Telemundo. There is so little pepper on the Hispanic tube that it is barely recognizable. In nearly ten years, I have never seen a Black Hispanic news anchor person or a Black Hispanic news reporter. I have never seen a Black Hispanic sports reporter or color analyst on either network. Both Telemundo and Univision produce materials and import materials from various other stations in Hispanic countries, and the story is the same inasmuch as Black involvement in the imported programs are concerned. There are almost zero Blacks in television ads, only a small dot of Blacks in Hispanic soap operas [telenovelas], and just as few in Hispanic movies. When Blacks manage to get roles in movies or telenovelas the roles are minor and/or degrading. Based on my observations, I would have to conclude that the Blacks in the Hispanic movie industry are much worse off than African-Americans in the movie industry in the United States.

If a Black plays a noticeable role in a white Hispanic production, that production reflects the racism that dominates Hispanic society. Themes such as forbidden love between a Black Hispanic and a white Hispanic, forbidden friendship between Black and white children, or the efforts of a very pale Black to "pass" for white are a few examples where a Black presence is felt. Even then, however, the Black projects his assimilation more than his Africanness, just as was the case in the United States until only recently. When it comes to sporting events, then one sees a few more African faces. The same is true of music-entertainment. But even in these type cases, the numbers are disproportionately low.

Speaking of music, let's take a glimpse of Hispanic radio in the Washington, D. C. metropolitan area. As of this writing, there are two major Hispanic radio stations here, WILC and WMDO. During all the time that I have monitored the Hispanic radio industry in this area, I can only recall three Black deejays who were on the air regularly. Does this suggest that there are few Blacks who are capable of being radio deejays? or does it suggest that they are being ignored by the white controlled Hispanic radio industry? Not surprisingly, the songs that are selected for airplay are overwhelmingly white-oriented. For the most part, Black musicians are ignored. The Black musicians who do manage to receive somewhat regular airplay cater to the commercial sound of white Hispanics for the most part. These include artists such as Celia Cruz or Oscar de Leon, for examples. Someone such as Mellow Man Ace or El General have to create a musical sensation in order to receive consistent airplay.

One can tune into Hispanic radio and regularly hear white Hispanic artists from Argentina, Venezuela, Chile, Mexico, Puerto Rico or any of the more than 20 Hispanic countries. Are We to believe that African Hispanics are not producing popular sounds that are just as commercial? or is this a situation that mirrors the music industry in the United States during the 1950s and 1960s. A Black teenager growing up in the United States in the 1950s and 1960s had to steadily move up and down the radio dial in order to find a song by a Black artist, and waited impatiently for the hour long shows that were set aside for Black music by white radio managers during their least listened to time slots. This certainly must be the major activity of Black Hispanic teens in Hispanic countries today who want to hear the hot sounds that are being produced by Black Hispanic musicians and who want to hear the Black deejay voices that are being ignored by the controllers of the Hispanic music industry.

If one picked up an Hispanic newspaper, one would see this same racist theme projecting itself. As a matter of fact, if you go by the pictures, you would wonder if there were any Black Hispanics doing anything newsworthy; that is, until you turned to the sports section. There you will have your best chance of seeing a Black face. The Hispanic press in Washington D. C. and the surrounding area reflects the concerns of white Hispanics. Black People, for the most part, are not a part of the production of the newspaper. The composition of the staffs is overwhelmingly white and the news coverage is outrageously white-dominated. Hispanic newspapers, in this area at least, do not reflect a healthy racial balance between Black Hispanics and white Hispanics.

As a rule, there are few Black political power players in Hispanic countries. If a Black person holds an important position in a Hispanic country, it is because there is a large concentration of Black People in that country. Otherwise, Hispanic political life is white political life. In fact, it is safe to say that the political system in the United States is less closed to African-Americans than the Hispanic system is to African-Hispanics.

But, enough of that; it is not the purpose of this essay to delve deeply into racism in Hispanic countries and among Hispanic peoples. That is a worthy subject that will some day get its proper due. However, it is important that this essay recognize the existence of Hispanic racism. Black People in the United States cannot afford to ignore this aspect of Hispanic society. We cannot afford to allow non-Blacks to trick Us into believing that there is hostility between African-Americans and white Hispanics because African-

Americans discriminate against Hispanics. That is certainly not the case! The fact of the matter is that white Hispanics come to the United States wrapped in a racist package. This racist package is slightly obscured in many Hispanic countries because the color classifications tend to merge among Hispanics, and no such merging exists in the United States. But this merging of "shades" does not eliminate the sinister element of race consciousness and racial discrimination. Race is just as powerful among white Hispanics as it is among white North Americans, white Germans, white Frenchmen, white Italians, white Portuguese, white Englishmen, white Spanishmen. When it comes to race, they are all essentially the same.

If you do not remember anything else from this essay, remember this: Every time a white Hispanic comes to this country, the number of white persons with racist tendencies in the United States of America increases by one!

I will begin by laying the foundation for the next couple of paragraphs. After those initial paragraphs, I will lay the foundation for this essay.

We are talking about four groups of persons here:

(1) The descendants of the Spanish who took the lands of South and Central America and sections of North America from the native inhabitants [so-called Indians];

(2) The descendants of the peoples who dominated South, Central and sections of North America before the Spanish arrived. These are the actual "Hispanic" (to the extent that this term is a legitimate one) people, a mixture of Spanish whites and native South and Central Americans who would be considered white insofar as

racial designations are applied in the United States today;

(3) Black People, descendants of sons and daughters of Africa who were enslaved in Spanish colonies after migrating to those colonies or being shipped there as slaves. These Blacks were dominated by the dominant Spanish culture and adopted the Spanish language; and

(4) Black People, descendants of sons and daughters of Africa who were enslaved in English speaking colonies in North America after migrating to those colonies or being shipped there as slaves. These Blacks were dominated by the dominant English culture and adopted the English language.

Let's be clear about the four groups of people we have mentioned. We have described:

(1) White Spaniards who colonized the Hispanic areas;

(2) White Hispanics who were the victims of that colonization;

(3) Black Hispanics [African-Hispanics] who are discriminated against because of their race; and

(4) Black People in the United States of America [African-Americans] who are victims of American discrimination because of their race.

There is a fifth group to consider. That group is white Americans and their leaders. This group despises Black People and Native Americans. Therefore, this group of white Americans despises Afro-Hispanics, African-Americans and Hispanic descendants of Native Americans.

As a consequence of the large migration of Hispanics into the United States, the two groups of Hispanics and the two groups of Blacks tend to find themselves trying to live in a neighborly way under less than desirable conditions. These undesirable conditions, collectively known as poverty, don't need to be characterized nor statistically verified because we all know what they are and how pervasive their negative impact on individuals is, but it is important that Hispanics and Blacks realize that their intermixing under these conditions is no accident. White Hispanic leaders in Central and South America realize that population decreases promote political stability in their troubled countries, and white political leaders in the United States realize that the importation of persons who will work for subsistence wages will increase the profits of white businessmen here. If these imported persons are non-Black and settle among Black Americans, they can serve the double purpose of curbing the gain in political influence African-Americans have been realizing since the 1950s. This political objective is extremely important to white Americans, who have convinced themselves that African-Americans and other Black People are the biggest threat to their security and way-of-life.

Thus, Hispanic leaders have what American leaders want (cheap, non-Black labor), and American leaders have what Hispanic leaders want (a dumping ground for unemployed and potential politically restless individuals). The white leaders talk on the telephones, meet in embassies, detail specifications, make deals, shake hands, make adjustments in their respective immigration laws and, just like that, the population of the United States explodes by millions. Most of these millions are non-Black individuals who can only afford to settle down in Black neighborhoods. That is where they are cleverly directed to seek housing, and that is where they end up.

Is it the fault of African-Americans or Hispanic immigrants that Hispanic immigrants end up in poverty-stricken neighborhoods? No, it is the fault of Hispanic leaders in Hispanic countries and white leaders in the United States. Is it the fault of African-Americans or Hispanic immigrants that they do not have enough positive information about each other to respect each other's culture, tradition, way-of-life, expectations and role as political pawns? No, it is the fault of Hispanic leaders in Hispanic countries and white leaders in the United States. Is it the fault of African-Americans or Hispanic immigrants that they can't communicate with each other (because of language problems) well enough to work through difficulties that normal human beings should be able to work through? No, it is the fault of Hispanic leaders in Hispanic countries and white leaders in the United States. Is it the fault of African-Americans or Hispanic immigrants that the two poverty stricken groups compete with each other for similar jobs? No, it is the fault of Hispanic leaders in Hispanic countries and white leaders in the United States. Is it the fault of African-Americans or Hispanic immigrants that Hispanic immigrants are willing to work for much smaller wages than African-Americans are willing to work for? No, it is the fault of Hispanic leaders in Hispanic countries and white leaders in the United States. Is it bad that Hispanic immigrants arrive here with relatively easy access to political and economic rights and privileges that African-Americans have fought centuries to attain? By all means not! African-Americans struggled for human rights, and all persons are entitled to them. And, is it the fault of African-Americans or Hispanic immigrants that Black People are discriminated against and forced to subsist in the poverty districts of the United States and Latin America? Of course not. There again, the fault lies outside of Hispanic immigrants and African-Americans. The fault lies with the white leaders and businessmen who benefit from Our condition. Therefore, if logic were to prevail, Hispanic immigrants and African-Americans would not be at each others' throat (if, in fact, that is the case), they would be jointly making plans to seize some of the power from the persons who manipulated them in the first place. To explore the possibility of such a union is what this essay proposes to do.

To begin with, we must discover what elements can serve as the basis of a political union within a group and between different groups of people. The fact that two groups are abused by the same enemy does not mean that those two groups can function as allies, not even temporarily. Logic suggests that that should be the case, but human tendencies have a way of making a joke of logic. What drives people, then, what pushes them into political motion, is the desire to acquire the goods and services they need and want. What frustrates nearly 100% of these same people is the fact that they have to institutionalize a process in order to satisfy that desire.

Put another way, people get involved in political activities because they want changes of an economic nature. Whether the objectives have an immediate or long range scope, they can always be reduced to basic economic arguments. Those individuals who want a change and, of their own free will, garner the energy and discipline needed to institutionalize a process that will serve their financial interests, are able to take advantage of those individuals who, for whatever reason, fail to do likewise. In the United States, white business entities have already institutionalized processes that serve their commercial interests. Since business is at the heart of their institutionalized processes, profits are revered more than peons (people) and moral principles. The issue with Black People and Hispanics in the United States, then, is this: Will their economic desires lead to the creation of institutionalized processes that can shake the status quo and satisfy the desires of its particular people? Have Black People in the United States advanced to that level of political maturity? Have Hispanics in the United States advanced to that level of political maturity? And, if so, have they founded their advance on principles that make them mutually compatible? We shall see.

African-Americans and Hispanic immigrants in the United States have quite a bit in common. They are both hard working and fun loving people. They both surround themselves with song, dance, romance and strong religious convictions and beliefs. The closer they are to their roots, to family and friends, the more secure they feel and act. They both view life in a balanced perspective, without the artificial constraints of puritan hypocrisy that splits the individual psyche of Euro-Americans. And, they both like to take care of business, but they don't want business to become so predominant that it turns life into a hell-bent rat race.

As a consequence of being colonized and enslaved, African-Americans and Hispanic immigrants have other characteristics in common. They are both devastated by poverty and inadequate economic opportunities. Drug addiction and alcoholism romp rampant through each community, manufacturing grotesque psychological scars and physical remnants of humanity gone to waste. They both are plagued by unemployment and hopelessness, and an abundance of religious nonsense is testimony that they believe that they are powerless to change their condition. They both spend disproportionate amounts of time in jail, while unwed and abandoned mothers rely on welfare, low-level jobs and night games to sustain tots and juveniles who don't have a chance of becoming successful in life. The overwhelming majority of the members of both groups live day-to-day by necessity, lacking this, lacking that, lacking other requisites; and they develop into teenagers and adults who are lacking in resolve, character and vision. The high technology equivalent of the proletariat? Look at African-Americans and Hispanic immigrants. Voila!

It can not escape anyone's attention that both African-Americans and Hispanics are natives of countries that American whites have traditionally viewed with disrespect and contempt. Western whites have taken liberties in African and Hispanic countries and with African and Hispanic leaders that can only be explained by superiority complex type theories. To American whites, the Hispanic national leaders across Central and South America have been a joke for nearly a century. African leaders had been regarded in even lower esteem. However, spurred by intellectual giants like W.E.B. DuBois and George Padmore and brilliant politicians and ideologists like Marcus Garvey and Patrice Lumumba, Africa took on more serious meaning to whites as Africa exploded on the international scene in the 1950s and 1960s, spearheading a power revolution within international organizations like the United Nations and in the minds of the world's decision makers. The reality of a bold, audacious and confrontational Africa that insisted on its own legitimacy forced westerners to make adjustments that they did not want to make, and made them fearful of Africa's independent potential. With fear came reluctant respect for Africans, and reluctant respect for Africa's diaspora. Latin America's leaders (other than Fidel Castro) have made no such impression on the leadership of the United States, and it reflects in the attitude white America has toward people of Hispanic ancestry.

It can't be just a co-incidence that white America always seeks cheap labor among people who are

NOT TO BE

militarily weak and less politically stable than westerners. How glaring the basic similarities are between the Hispanic immigrants of today and the sons and daughters of Africa more than 400 years ago! Hispanic immigrants are preferred, then, because of their <u>similarities</u> to African-Americans, similarities that white America feels make Hispanics "safe." Think about this, because it will be re-explored later.*

African-Americans and Hispanic immigrants in the United States share another "distinction." Psychologically speaking, they both have what white people are missing and so dearly want— color. It has yet to be determined how the absence of color has impacted on the psyche of white people, and how this impact manifests itself in the conduct of white people toward people of color. The reality of color, however, its presence and its absence, cannot be taken lightly. After all, color is that element without which there is very little cosmetic variety and even less physical beauty, and both African-Americans and Hispanics have a noticeable supply of it. Whether it can serve as an additional focal point for political unity between the two is doubtful, but it might be of some value somewhere down the line.**

Color long ago took value within the white American status quo. Proof of that is in the fact that both African-Americans and Hispanic immigrants are discriminated against based on physical appearance. African-Hispanics, as they should, assume what is African-American when they arrive in the United States and move in, out, and about the country. Their color, not the language they speak, is what essentially defines them; and they are accepted as is, as equal components, by the African-American community. Non-Black Hispanic immigrants, for the most part, are easily distinguishable from their pale North American hosts. Their appearance precedes them, categorizes them, pre-sorts them and predetermines their abilities and limitations. If a decent job is at stake and all other check points are fairly equal, the African-American and Hispanic immigrant will likely be "done in" by his or her physical appearance. As Black People have learned, how one responds to this internally is much more important, politically, than his or her apparent response.

African-Americans have already overcome the language barrier, but that barrier still retards the progress of Hispanic immigrants. Quite importantly, it impedes the ability of the two groups to communicate clearly. Additionally, African-Americans have managed to merge as one people after having arrived here from several different nations on the African continent. Hispanic immigrants are still arriving from several different countries, and they are holding onto their national allegiances. The ideas of Hispanitud and Hispanic Unity are being broadcast on the Hispanic networks in the United States, plugged by various entertainers, written about by media people and propagandists and pushed by certain Hispanic government spokespersons and big business interests, but it is a hard sell to persons who have traditionally and most recently considered themselves Peruvian, Guatemalan, Chilean, Cuban or any of twenty other nationalities. Even though they all speak basically the same language (dialects vary, sometimes drastically), practice the same religion and have a great deal else in common, they view fellow nationals in one regard and non-nationals in a different regard. The Hispanic immigrants in the United States will eventually think of themselves primarily as Hispanic-Americans and loosen their nationalist ties, but that is still a few generations down the line. Hispanic Unity, at this time, is more a commercial push than a political one; the

NOT TO BE

effort of big business interests who want to organize the Hispanic people in order to more effectively exploit them money-wise and labor-wise. If it continues as such, Hispanic Unity will not mean much at all to most Hispanic Americans because commercial interests will sell off the average Hispanic individual and principle every time. African-Americans have learned that lesson. Unfortunately, African-Americans have not made the called for adjustments. Hispanics beware!

It is apparent to even a casual observer that the Hispanic immigrants in this country prefer to be around African-Americans rather than white Americans. Maybe it would be more accurate to say that Hispanic Americans prefer the African-American lifestyle over the white American lifestyle. It is almost as if the African-American lifestyle is not foreign to them, and I can feel why. Take away the physical differences between African-Americans and white Americans, and the basic differences between the two are easily discernible. Take away the physical differences between African-Americans and Asian-Americans, and the basic differences between the two are easily discernible. Take away the physical differences between African-Americans and Arab-Americans, and the basic differences between the two are easily discernible. The same is true of African-Americans and Japanese-Americans, Americans from India and other non-Black immigrants to America. But, take away the physical differences between African-Americans and Hispanic immigrants in America, and the basic differences appear so minor that one might be tempted to disregard them. These two groups of people have a lot more in common than they think! They share intangibles. Maybe it's a consequence of being colonized by Europeans, but I suggest it is also because, at some time long ago, the ancestors of these two peoples got to know each other very, very well.

But, if that were the case, it was then. It does not necessarily speak to anything as regards the here and now, but it is definitely food for thought.

As is all that has been said to this point. But, what does all of this lead to? So what if African-Americans and Hispanic Americans are both victims of white political and business interests? So what if they came to this land from countries and governments that white Americans traditionally feel contempt for? So what if they both came to this land from several different countries and backgrounds that served as impediments to unity within each group? So what if they both are people of color, are discriminated against on the basis of physical appearance and share some profound intangible similarities? What do these factors suggest about the probability of African-American and Hispanic political unity within the United States arena? Is that prospect probable? Some would argue so, others not. My conclusions follow.

ASIDES

* p. 27 [The reasons that really explain why Black People were enslaved is explored in detail in Ten Lessons: An Introduction to Black History, edited by Mbulu and Sekou and published in 1993 by "The People."]
**p. 27 [The relationship of color to health is yet to be realized. It must, at some point, be probed.]

NOT TO BE

Conclusion

Why were Hispanics selected to fulfill America's cheap labor needs? Why not Asians, or Arabs, or Pacific Islanders? Why not other whites, from western or eastern Europe? Why Hispanics? Simply because Hispanics are more like African-Americans than any of the other mentioned peoples.

But alike how? Shouldn't similarities increase the possibilities of African-Americans and Hispanics uniting against white American discrimination and domination? If those were the type similarities whites had observed, white businessmen and politicians definitely would not have recruited Hispanics and placed them right in the midst of African-Americans. The similarities that appealed to white leaders were the type that suggest that Hispanic immigrants would fail to be politically astute to the point where they could become a threat to the white American way-of-life. America's white leadership concluded that Hispanics, like African-Americans, would not develop a sophisticated enough degree of political maturity to orchestrate an independent political platform or unite with their "natural" allies and force the changes that they feel are necessary. If their assessment is correct, then African-Americans and Hispanics in the United States will not form a viable political bloc. They will, instead, grow continually more hostile toward each other and possibly render each other politically ineffective.

Is the assessment of the white leadership a legitimate one? Of course it is. Will the actual reaction of Hispanics and African-Americans play out the way the white leaders have anticipated? Only time will tell, but developments up to now indicate as much. But before delving into this latter point, let's delve into the former, that of the legitimacy of the white assessment.

Using western standards as a yardstick, one must conclude that Hispanics and African-Americans are immature inasmuch as political development is concerned. The definitive African-American political statement, that of Black Nationalism [as espoused by the Republic of New Afrika], is largely an underachievement. It is an underachievement because the masses of African-Americans do not have the resolve nor inclination to intimate that concept, and the educated African-Americans, the African-American "leadership pool", lacks the daring, initiative and confidence needed to advance that concept. What is left then is "Black Power", which, like Hispanic or Latino Unity, is much too vaguely enunciated to promote mature political progress. As a matter of fact, neither "Black Power" nor Latino Unity is a product of astute political forethought. They are both reactions well after the fact of being politically and/or militarily dominated. The only political activity African-Americans and Hispanics have demonstrated a knack for is civil rights-integration. Unfortunately, such an objective is incapable of bringing about the type changes that are necessary if African-Americans and Hispanics are to attain genuine equality in the United States.

A sentiment that does not exist of its own energy can not take a group of dominated people very far. That is exactly where African-Americans and Hispanics come up short. African-American Unity— is it actually felt, actually desired? or is it the absence of being accepted by white Americans as equals that African-Americans feel? Ditto with Hispanics. Do they really desire Latino Unity? Do they really want to create a better social structure? Or was their primary concern resolved when they escaped a quality of life that was absolutely abominable? Answers to questions such as these lurk

NOT TO BE

deep inside of millions of individuals and subconsciously dictate what an individual is willing to do and how much of his/her dreams he/she is willing to sacrifice.

White leaders have bet the house that the personal desires and aspirations of African-Americans and Hispanics will help prevent the two from effectively uniting. White leaders are betting that the two groups, neither singly nor together, will prove capable of elaborating and sustaining the creative energy and dedication needed to radically change America. The images of prosperity, the prospect of dollars and cents and material gratifications, the myths of equal opportunity and democracy and the conscience-cleansing powers of "talking a good game"; all of these factors and others like them will conspire to break down the traditional values and morals of people and put them up for sale—

WANTED
**People to cherish America
And share the American dream.
Prospects outstanding, Sky the limit!
This is your chance to be all that you can be.**

In order for African-Americans and Hispanics to form an effective political bloc, they must overcome the appeal of America's promises, the power of her images. They must be willing to settle for a decent life and put the images of an exaggerated lifestyle to scorn. Each group must feel and elaborate its own objectives, and not let their struggle be reduced to white America's favorite slogans. If each group can determine its own priorities, that will constitute a first step toward political maturity. But that will not serve the purpose as long as each group's leaders are eager to switch to pay-off mode

The Hispanic Factor 33

when white America calls.

All indications point to the probability that the Hispanic experience in the United States will be an accelerated version of the African-American struggle of the last half century. Moreover, educated and skilled Hispanics will receive support from elements of the status quo that African-Americans never received. The masses of African-Americans and Hispanics have already realized that it makes sense for the two to unite, but the masses generally have not had the resolve necessary to institutionalize what they have realized makes sense. Moreover, American democracy is not a mass-oriented democracy, but a democracy of special interests that corrupts and employs the talents of those who are prepared to serve them well. This factor, added to all that was said earlier (Hispanic racism, communications barriers, promises and images of personal prosperity, loss of traditional values and morals, loss of allegiance, political immaturity, etc.) will make African-American and Hispanic unity a probable liability for both groups.

Both African-Americans and Hispanics should be very careful. The two groups are alike in too many dangerous ways, too many ways that can be exploited by a slick white leadership. There are some explosively delicate parameters involved in an African-American/Hispanic political union, and either of the parameters could experience a slight or sudden disequilibrium, turn the two groups against each other, and leave white America sitting prettier and more in control than ever.

white

people

don't

read

black

books

What are the possibilities of real integration in the United States of America. Have white Americans in fact changed their attitudes and outlook toward Black People?

CONTENTS:

Introduction

As a general rule, I would suggest that there is no love lost between Black People and white people in the United States of America. The history that the two groups share represents a perpetual condition of antagonistic contact, and it is now as much metaphysical as openly expressed. Nonetheless, each group has developed its own "comfort zone" as regards this contact. Even though the social tensions continue to grow in leaps and bounds, individually we reluctantly accept each other's humanity (some in lesser degrees than others). It is based on this reluctant acceptance, this drop of sanity in a sea of antagonism and malcontent, that this essay is written.

A profile of both groups, including the components of both groups, is necessary. We will view each in terms of power, perception, status and accommodation. First though, I will take one paragraph to comment on both groups in terms of intelligence.

All persons possess equal intelligence capacities. The degree to which each person's intelligence is developed is determined by mostly external conditions (in the absence of a genetic abnormality). White people and Black People in the United States are widely exposed to essentially the same phenomena, but in different (sometimes widely different) degrees and under different circumstances. The bottom line is that both groups, individually and collectively, are "learned." However, white people's "learning" (intelligence developed) is frequently short-circuited by more powerful racist tendencies, while Black People's "learning" (intelligence developed) is frequently short-circuited by their desire to be recognized and accepted by white people as equals. Consequently, when the two groups interact, it is impossible to predict what role, if any, intelligent objectivity will play in that interaction. An unstable response is just as probable as any other.

Power

Power is the ability to define terms, including the willingness to mold society and take on the ultimate responsibility for so doing. Power is the ability to control; it is the ability to determine the fate of others.

White people love to wield power. They love to be decision makers because that enables them to chart a course that will hopefully ensure their personal and group well-being. If, while making decisions, other individuals and groups suffer disproportionately, well, "that's the price of progress." After all, "self-preservation is the first law of nature" and "survival of the fittest" is nature's way of weeding out the "weak" elements and ensuring the prevalence of the human species.

Individually, the power element dominates white relationships. White men dominate white women, while white women map out a strategy that will eventually enable them to dominate white men (they hope). White bosses dominate their employees, while white employees hope for the day when they can be the boss and bark out the orders. White business persons attempt to dominate their competitors, white politicians attempt to dominate/destroy their political rivals, white parents dominate their children, et cetera. In white relationships, power hovers everywhere. It is the hidden element, the unspoken but clearly understood advantage, the tie breaker, the always accessible ace in the hole. Power is always there, and white individuals are accustomed to its presence.

Collectively, which group (or nation, or race, etc.)

wields power is so important to white people that they can not imagine sharing power with others. Naturally, it follows that they can not bear the thought of having less power than others, or of being powerless. But, because white individuals had demonstrated a tendency to ruthlessly abuse power, the writers of the United States Constitution took political power out of the hands of individuals and put it into offices and institutions. This measure met the approval of whites at the time it was enacted because the understanding was that only white men would occupy the offices. White individuals were to compete with other white individuals periodically for the right to wield power. Whoever won would be obligated to act in the interest of white people and tolerated if he acted in his own interest within unspecified but understood limitations.

In short, what has been stated is the following. White individuals are accustomed to the influence and presence of power in their personal relationships; white people expect wielders of power to act in the interest of the white collective; and white people expect wielders of power to use that power to bolster his/her personal estate.

Power was not a factor in the individual lives of Black People in America insofar as Blacks relating to other Blacks was concerned. Point blank, Black individuals had no control over how they lived and no control over how any other person lived. White people, individually and collectively, had that control; in the roles of master, officeholder, citizen and legally recognized person. All of them and each of them forced Black individuals and Black People to experience power from the receiving end of a whip and while looking down the wrong end of a barrel. Power, to Black People in the United States, was a one-sided coin, and that side held the imprint of a merciless caucasian.

But Black People's responses to white power were not one-sided. For passive Blacks and those who could "make-do" regardless of extenuating conditions, it meant the begrudging acceptance of white people as the wielders of power and coming to acknowledge that as the norm. For Black rebels and freedom fighters, it meant a desire for vengeance. Sure, these individuals wanted liberty, equality and self-government, etc., but they also wanted vengeance for the abuse and shame that had been heaped upon them. Slaughtering white people while in the act of rebelling would bring them a measure of satisfaction, a political orgasm, that nothing else could possibly bring. For the most part, this realization of Black Power was not to be.

As African-Americans evolved, their intimate relationships began to resemble white intimate relationships in that African-American men tended to abuse and dominate African-American women based on financial considerations. African-Americans imitated whites, to be sure, but the actual power that was wielded was infantile; it was not supported by laws, it was not institutionalized, it was not weaved into the minds, hearts and establishments of the status quo. The power that was present in white people's individual relationships can be likened to a 9mm semi-automatic pistol. By comparison, the power in Black individual relationships can only be likened to an air gun.

It can be asserted that African-Americans fear power. They fear power because power is so easily abused and because African-Americans are not willing to take on the ultimate responsibility of initiating measures that could cause large numbers of persons to suffer disproportionately. Thus, like the writers of the constitution, African-Americans seek alternatives to individual power wielding. African-Americans prefer power by committee, a preference that is misinterpreted by whites, who equate it to acquiescence.

We can go further. The reluctance of African-Americans to assume ultimate responsibility equates to an African-American preference for white wielders of power. Since whites have traditionally wielded power, African-Americans accord them a taste of political deference. Thus, even when an African-American assumes an office, he or she seeks white input and tries to wield power in a way that meets the approval of white people. Whites discriminatively interpret this as incompetence.

What all of this reduces to is the following: African-Americans view white people as capable, but abusive. White people view African-Americans as less than competent, indecisive and, above all, untrustworthy (the color factor).

Perception

Perception is the intuitive understanding of your "place". It is, according to Webster, "physical sensation in the light of experience." Perception determines whether one has the desire to stand out. Perception determines whether one has the desire to wield power.

White people conceive themselves as leaders and components of a superior group of people. In spite of the fact that, psychologically speaking, white people feel a profound deficiency within themselves, they feel their natural role is to organize, make decisions and issue instructions. They are so visibly confident in this perception because they are fed a constant diet of white mythology that ignores their deficiencies and champions their strengths and accomplishments. This mythology allows for horizontal and vertical comparisons of white people with other white people, but only vertical comparisons of white people with non-white people (with whites on top, naturally). Even if the eyes, ears and intelligence of white individuals tell them that a horizontal comparison of whites to non-whites is justified and appropriate, these individuals will refuse to compare accordingly until white institutions, the purveyors of white mythology,* place their stamp of approval on such a comparison.

Black People perceive themselves as important but relatively minor parts of a group. The Black mythology, though estranged from the conscious environments of African-Americans for centuries, is still part of Our sub-conscious life force. It tends to promote exclusively horizontal comparisons of people, regardless of race or color. The Black mythology is a balanced mythology. Black individuals do not go into a set of circumstances thinking that they are "better" than non-Black individuals. This does not, however, exclude the probability that many Black individuals would have preferences based on what they are accustomed to.

African-Americans are hardly aware of who they are, but their "place" has been firmly entrenched in their conscious minds for nearly four centuries. African-Americans have heard white America's dictates for hundreds of years and have conformed, but African-Americans have not been convinced. African-Americans know that they are not inferior in any way, but they do not know how to act out or project this reality to themselves and the world at large. The world at large takes note of this uncertainty, misinterprets its basis, and disparagingly categorizes Blacks accordingly.**

Thus, perception-wise, white people perceive themselves as leaders and observe uncertainty in what African-Americans project about themselves (African-

NOT TO BE

Americans). African-Americans, on the other hand, view themselves as part of a whole. They want to assert their equality, but they do not want to generate any "problems" while doing so.

ASIDES

* p. 42 [It, this white mythology, can only be cracked by non-white people because white people are not equipped to do so; white people can not, of their own accord, replace the white mythology in their hearts and minds with the white reality. This mythology can only be cracked by non-white people who either dominate whites militarily (it is not the purpose of this essay to discuss warfare) or take every opportunity available to provide white people with constant reminders of their humane deficiencies and the horrible consequences of their reign as world "leaders". Up to this point, non-whites, particularly African-Americans (in the United States of America), have been unwilling to feed white people this diet they so critically need in order to restore balance to their perception. This is what persons like Malcolm X, George Jackson, John Brown and Louis Farrakan intuitively understood— that whites have to be forced to face up to their misdeeds, their inhumanities; that they have to be virtually shamed into "fessin up" because pampering the message leaves the white mythology uncracked, unaffected, in tact.]

** p. 42 [That African-Americans have uncertainties about how to assert their equality is a prime example of intelligence gone astray. All We need to be is Ourselves, and equality will be acknowledged. But that thought, the thought of being Ourselves, is short-circuited and re-transmitted into "How can African-Americans get the recognition of white Americans?" It is this question that gives birth to expressions of uncertainty.]

Status

Again, let us refer to Webster. Status is "relative rank in a hierarchy of prestige." Since prestige is not necessarily a consequence of logical analysis nor common sense assessment, status goes beyond what seems to be the case or what should be the case. Status represents what is actually the case, what is at the core of the case. Status is somewhat beyond "the condition of a person or thing in the eyes of the law;" status is the condition of a person or thing in the spirit of the law and in the hearts and souls of "significant others." Status is real, but we must remember that its development and asignment is quite fickle and arbitrary.

We are not speaking of individuals here. When it comes to the issue of race, status is beyond the individual. To wit, white Americans are the founding fathers, the authors of the Declaration of Independence and the Constitution, the pioneers of westward expansion. When Europe faltered, white Americans held the western world together and forged onward with new technologies into new spaces. White Americans envisioned, white Americans went, white Americans saw, white Americans dominated. In addition, all the great thinkers, the great planners, the great warriors, the great doers, the great aesthetics; all were white. That is the white mythology, and therein lies the status that beams across the country and illuminates the consciousness of white individuals.

African-Americans, in the true spirit of the law and in the hearts and souls of significant others, are "3/5 of a man," fugitives from slavery, aptitude-deficient escapees from Africa, the dark continent. Tarzan, wild animals, thick jungles, pygmies, alligators, murderous rapids— stir them all together and, there it is; Us; Us African-Americans, Us Hispanic Africans, Us African Caribs, Us Aborigines, Us whatever. Us, purely subjective, since all is intuitively assumed and understood. Our status is Us.

As such, white people do not "see" Black People; **they have not been forced to recognize** Us. When We challenge white people, We challenge them as integrationists, civil rightists or "wannabes"— but never as Black People **who happen to be** in America. We don't confront them as Africans or New Afrikans, as culturally and politically distinct entities. As a consequence, white people are more suspicious of revelations of Black accomplishments than they are of revelations of any other group of people. To white Americans, Black People (African-Americans included) are the most marginal members of society, afterthoughts at best, who rarely contribute anything of their own; and whites therefore automatically reject the thought of Black status. African-Americans, on the other hand, have been fed the white mythology for centuries. Even though African-Americans know this mythology is replete with lies and half-truths, only the best are able to resist it. Most succumb to it. Even when most African-Americans talk about whites in critical terms, they effectively validate white status by imitating whites and allowing whites to dictate the conditions under which African-Americans and white Americans relate to each other.

Whenever, wherever, white status is unquestioned. Whenever, wherever, Black status is unconfirmed. White people never approve of anything Black without first making it their own, without forcing changes that make it "acceptable." African-Americans, by contrast, accept what whites have to offer without imposing any conditions. That contrast says it all.

[It does not take much intestinal fortitude to sell out; to submit to others without imposing any conditions. That is exactly what many African-Americans do, particularly the huge majority of those who consider themselves "successful" and representative of the "best" Black America has to offer. These individuals go from day to day imitating and approximating images beamed to them by white America, and accomplish practically nothing that will be remembered beyond their days of useful employment. Yet they think they have more going for them than the so-called "average" Black person.

The fact of the matter probably is that the best individuals Black America has to offer are rarely "successful" because they are unwilling to accept a Black-white relationship based on white America's dictates. They value themselves too much for that, and prefer to live on a subsistence income or a life of crime rather than live as a relatively comfortable chump.

There are no Toussaint L'Ouvertures to be found among chumps and imitators; no Harriet Tubmans, no Dan Freemans, no Nzingas. In spite of the appearances, there is nothing of substance to that type of "success".]

Accommodation

The concept of accommodation refers to a frame of mind, a spiritual disposition, that acknowledges the rights, privileges and humanity of others. To accommodate is to concede, to defer, to recognize that the humanity of others is just as valid as your own.

Accommodation is a critical element because it promotes goodwill between diverse groups that need to work in harmony toward commonly beneficial ends, and because it can act as a safeguard against the abusive wielding of power. The spirit of accommodation generates an air of equality and trust, and sedates suspicions that one group might harbor about the "real" and underlying motives of other groups. Since every group has some legitimate concerns, a spirit of accommodation can help assure that each group's concerns are addressed as appropriately as possible.

We have seen earlier that white people are power-oriented. Power-oriented people concede nothing and disdain accommodation (and accommodationists). To submit as a consequence of superior opposition, as a consequence of being overwhelmed; that is understandable and acceptable. But to submit because of a sense of justice is a sign of weakness and an indication that one is not mentally tough enough to take a hard stand and see it through to realization. Such is the thinking of power-oriented people.

Black People have traditionally been an accommodating people. That is why Our history of relating to other races of people, even when We were militarily superior, produced goodwill and mutually beneficial consequences. And then the white man came! By the time Black People arrived on America's shores, We had experienced so many centuries of being harassed and abused by white people that seeking to accommodate them was out of the question.

Thus, in the face of white America, the early options of Black People were limited to either resisting or surrendering. After a couple of centuries of resisting, Black People surrendered [See "We Changed"]. For the most part, Black People maintained that posture until persons such as Marcus Garvey and movements such as Pan-Africanism led Us to re-assess Our position. That re-assessment re-awakened the concept of Black Power, placed it smack in the middle of the dialogue of African-

Americans, and made it possible for African-Americans to assume an accommodationist posture when it is deemed practical.

African-Americans have not accommodated white America (white power has overwhelmed Blacks in this country), but they are eager to do so. Whites are aware of this, as they are aware of Our accommodationist tradition. What African-Americans don't realize is that whites see accommodation as an expression of weakness. A quality that represents a human strength is thus misinterpreted as a weakness by whites, and the people who demonstrate that quality are underestimated as a result.

In short, whites know that African-Americans will settle for much less than African-Americans deserve. Their read is that African-Americans are prone to defer or sacrifice a principle, and whites do not recognize the value of that. Nor do they respect it.

Summary

In a nutshell, what has been said to this point is the following:

(1) White people are accustomed to the omnipresence of power. White people love to wield power and love to mingle and scheme with wielders of power. White people have observed that African-Americans are reluctant to wield power, even when African-Americans assume positions of power. White people assume that this reluctance is a consequence of lack of confidence and incompetence, and devalue African-Americans as a result. Even in 1994 this is true, in spite of what white people promulgate to the contrary.

(2) White people perceive themselves as leaders of the world, sense that African-Americans perceive white

people as leaders and sense that African-Americans perceive African-Americans as something less. The African-American insistence on imitating whiteness instead of asserting Blackness transmits a more powerful, underlying message-- that African-Americans do not hold themselves nor their culture in as high regard as African-Americans hold white people and white culture. The bottom line subconscious read that white people get is that African-Americans are not quite up to the task yet.

(3) African-Americans do not insist on confirming their status as Black People. African-Americans will agree to whatever changes necessary if those changes will result in white people's stamp of approval. With African-Americans disposed to act as such, white people are never confronted with a reason to respect what African-Americans have to offer. The thinking of whites could well be, "Why should whites respect what African-Americans seem so eager to rid themselves of?" Ergo, whites do not respect what Blacks have to offer.

(4) White people know that African-Americans will settle for much less than they deserve, as long as African-Americans get the seeming approval of white people. African-American integrationists and civil rights leaders are harshly criticized by Black Nationalists for the positions they take, but they are ridiculed even more cruelly behind doors that enclose only white individuals. White Americans know just as well as Black People when African-American leaders voice and write opinions that are incorrect and out of contact with Black priorities. Whites don't publicly criticize African-American leaders when they take such positions because white people are the benefactors of those positions, but privately they talk and probably joke about the cowardice and incompetence of such persons, and denigrate them and all African-Americans as a result.

From all of this emerges a formula that should be crystal clear to all of us.

White people's ideas about power

+

White people's ideas about perception

+

White people's ideas about status

+

White people's ideas about accommodation

=

White people don't value Black People

=

"White People Don't Read Black Books".

What does that title mean, what is at the root of it, and why does it even matter? We will see in the conclusion to this essay.

NOT TO BE

Conclusion

The textbooks that America's elementary, secondary and high school children read are not the works of Black persons, nor do they represent Black People in a positive light. The same is true of the colleges, where we might find a Black History course that uses a book authored by a Black person whose perspective is not threatening to whites. But philosophy, psychology, mathematics, the sciences, etc., are subjects that represent the works of white individuals. As a matter of fact, pupils in American schools are more apt to read a textbook by an Asian, other Easterner or European than a Black person. That represents the mentality of white people in regards to the intelligence of Black People.

Many are the reasons that suggest why whites don't read Black books— whites don't grow up exposed to Black works, whites cannot easily access Black works and whites are led to believe that Blacks cannot "deliver the goods" at a high enough level; and whites grow up learning to deprecate and disparage that which is Black. No matter what the subject, whites think a Black person will not analyze it sufficiently, and whites will suppose that there is some data, some arcane information of the utmost relevance, that a white person will take into account that will not be accounted for by a Black person.

Whites who consider themselves "educated" might even feel that others will judge them by what they are known to read. If we are (corporeally) what we eat, then we are also (intellectually) what we read. In this society, it would follow that those who read Black writings (and take them seriously) would be stigmatized and regarded in a lower glow than those who toe the white line. With financial considerations being what they are, those who toe the white line are likely to be better compensated and given more opportunities for compensation than those who do not.

One thing is certain. The education/media establishment, those individuals, associations and organizations that are the standard bearers of the white mythology, know that there is an inherent risk in Black authors. These persons know that after the logic and facts begin to point toward "undesirable" conclusions, conclusions that do not speak well of white people, white researchers and white authors will intuitively cloud the logic and facts and allow the white mythology to determine what is actually written or exposed to the public. Black writers are less likely to be attached to the "scholarly demands" that come with being white, and therefore cannot be trusted to deliver a message that will re-enforce the metaphysical infrastructure of white individuals. Since one's metaphysical infrastructure is so very important, the white standard bearers are reluctant to approve of and/or promulgate writers whose tendency would be to criticize whites and question the validity of white people's racial- and self- concepts.

But this is exactly what African-Americans who seek the recognition of whites and integration with whites need to be doing, and they need to be doing it without equivocation and without trying to make this pill of reality easier for white people to swallow. If African-Americans do not force white Americans to listen to the truth about themselves and face up to their shortcomings as leaders and human beings, white Americans will never respect African-Americans nor grant that African-Americans are of the proper status to merit integration with whites. And it is at this point, precisely, that we begin to understand what the title of this essay, "White People don't Read Black Books," actually represents.

Integrationists, civil rightists, multiculturalists of

whatever race or genre, take heed! As long as white Americans refuse to view you as an equal, there can not be any genuine civil rights nor genuine integration nor genuine multicultural melting pot. The chances that white people will accept non-white peoples, particularly Blacks, as equals are slim at best; but they are impossible as long as white people continue to hang onto that primitive mindset that is a product of the white mythology. Those who want to integrate with white people and culturally merge with white people must first destroy the white mythology that is at the core of everything white people learn.

No more appeasing white people! No more slipping them tiny, indirect doses of what they need in order to progress with all deliberate speed. The message, instead, must be rammed down their throats. Everywhere white people look and listen, they must see and hear African-Americans talking about the white reality, not the white mythology; and they must hear this message exactly as it is, without any sugar coating. This is the only way [short of violence, and we are not discussing violence in this essay] white people will take the message of African-Americans seriously. As we approach the 21st century, white people are not yet developed enough to think objectively about themselves or their actions. Sugar coating the criticisms of them allows them to maintain their way of thinking in tact, to continue to rationalize their cruel and discriminatory modus operandi, and to hear the criticisms without taking them seriously. But to give it to them straight upsets them, puts them on the defensive, and produces small cracks in their white mythological armor. These cracks will raise the possibility that white persons can be forced to question the veracity of the white mythology. Within these cracks lay the only hope that African-Americans can re-educate white people (properly this time) and make them fit enough to take seriously and participate in objectives such as integration and multiculturalism.

White Americans are in leadership positions but they are not developed enough to lead. Non-white peoples must let this recognition guide them. The equivalent of a four or five year old brat is running the family business, and all of the family's members are suffering as a result. The adult members of the family have to take control of this brat, diminish his role and properly socialize him. Otherwise, the odds are that he will never develop into a fit, mature member of the family.

That is how it should be, but that is not the present state of relations. In the present, the today and now, the formula is as was stated earlier in this essay. To wit,

White people's ideas about power
+
White people's ideas about perception
+
White people's ideas about status
+
White people's ideas about accommodation
=
White people don't value Black People
=
"White People Don't Read Black Books".

Are there any white individuals who read Black books? Sure there are, but their motives for doing so are debatable (in most cases) and they don't read Black authors with the same open, trusting and objectively analytical mind with which they read white authors. By now, this thought should be easy for readers of this essay to process. To make sure We all understand, let's paraphrase the above formula this way.

White people don't read Black books

=

White people don't take Black People's intelligence
seriously

=

White people don't respect Black People

=

Integration is out of the question.

A combination of assimilation-genocide is what white America is prepared to contribute to the integrationist aspirations of African-Americans and other multi-culturalists of color. Not a whit more! We should be intelligent enough to keep that in mind and act accordingly.

we

changed

An important and revealing account of the process that changed Africans who were shipped to this country as slaves into African-Americans. This historical essay explains how the change came about and when it actually began to exert itself.

CONTENTS:

Introduction

We changed. Black People in the United States changed. Enough of this Afro-centric rhetoric that continually floods from Our mouths! Enough of these "Black is Beautiful" and "Black and Proud" type proclamations! We are Black, certainly, but We do not consider Ourselves beautiful because We prefer to judge beauty from the perspective of "white." We prefer to do that! And proud? Sure, We have managed to convince Ourselves that We are proud, and We are in a superficial way. But proud of the fact of Our Blackness? I don't think so. Proud, yes, but proud in spite of Our Blackness. Proud in spite of submitting to white domination. Proud, because to be less than proud would result in the total collapse of Our psychological infrastructure. Proud because We could not look Ourselves in the mirror, We could not keep Our knees from buckling under, if We admitted otherwise.

Black People in the United States want to be American more than anything else in the world. If white people would only "act right", We would reduce Our cultural and political ties to Africa to an absolute minimum. And We would do it in a New York minute! Our ancestors, the Black People who were brought to this continent as slaves, would have recoiled at the mere thought.

We changed. Black People in the United States changed for the worse. How did this change come about, why did it come about, and, most importantly, when did this change take place. This brief essay will attempt to answer these questions.

I. The Colonial Years: African Dominance

The Black persons who were brought to this continent in the 1500s and 1600s were proud of who they were. They had dignity, pride, self-respect; and they were accustomed to self-government, equality of rights and opportunity and a general condition of justice. They were more intelligent than present-day Black Americans, mentally tougher, more stable psychologically, physically superior and culturally attached. And, they had more common sense than present-day Black Americans. They were more desperate, so they trusted their instincts to the max, and their instincts were clear and sharp when it came to white people— whites were the enemy, whites meant Us no good, whites were never to be trusted.

Definitely, the Africans who came to this country during the colonial years had their defense mechanisms in tact. Their response to white people was automatic, instinctual, primal; there was only one set of parameters, one response, one solution. White people had invaded their land, disrupted their homes and destroyed their families. White people had shattered whatever tranquility Our ancestors had managed to accumulate, disrespected their culture and tradition, enslaved them and left their bodies either homeless and unprotected or dead. When it came to white people, no thought was necessary, no process of analysis and evaluation was required. The reaction was automatic. White people were the enemy and their control over Our lives had to be brought to an end.

From the 1600s through the Revolutionary War period (1790s), African-Americans planned and executed hundreds and hundreds of revolts against white power. These revolts have been called slave rebellions, but those Black revolutionaries did not have a slave mentality. Nor

NOT TO BE

were they trying to force the white establishment to make humanitarian adjustments in regard to Black People. They did not take to the streets in the form of a riot. They did not march in protest. They did not plead for better treatment or improved housing conditions. They did not demand fair judicial treatment. They did not run away, kill whites, break hoes, set the plantations on fire, unite with the Indians, poison white people or spit in their food because they wanted white people to make humanitarian concessions. Early Africans in America carried out revolutionary activities because they wanted self-government, liberty, real equality*. They wanted to recapture what had been taken away from them; anything less than that, anything other than that, was not even being considered.

Even the minor acts of revolt were not intended to make white people change. The poison, the spit, the broke hoes and field fires, were meant to mete out spiteful revenge, to instill fear in whites, to weaken white people and set them up for larger, more pervasive acts of revolution. There was no desire to use the same toilet white people used, to eat at the same table white people ate at, or sit at a desk side by side with white children and white adults. None of that! None of that because none of that was fundamental. Without the power to enact and enforce laws, none of that meant anything of value to Black People, and the colonial period Africans in America recognized as much.

This was not only true of the Blacks who had been enslaved. The so-called "free" blacks were of the same mind. Their "freedom" was a farce, and they realized it. For that reason, the "free" Africans participated in the revolts just as avidly as did the enslaved Africans. The "free" Blacks plotted and schemed against white people in major and minor ways just as did the enslaved Blacks.

The "free" Blacks, like the enslaved Blacks, acted in ways that would promote Black self-determination and maintained attitudes that were consistent with that objective. They were not interested in sugar coated concessions, bombastic promises or empty appearances. They already had that, as their "free" status indicated. What they wanted was the real thing, what had been taken away from them. They wanted to control their own lives, they wanted to control their own destiny, they wanted to control.

The maroons were Africans who ran away from the plantations in search of freedom and self-government. These runaway slaves banded together in the mountains, the swamps, wherever they could, and established their own laws of conduct and survival. In effect, they established Black provisional and temporary governments that made all of the social, political, educational, judicial and economic decisions that were of primary concern to them. They raided surrounding plantations not to force the whites to treat Blacks right, but in order to obtain goods and recruits that were needed to keep the provisional Black Nation functioning. They fought against the white militias that tracked them down not because they couldn't live as slaves, but because they refused to live as slaves, as powerless men and women. They sent spies onto the plantations and into the towns in order to arouse the revolutionary sentiments of the Blacks there, not because they were interested in undermining white people but because they wanted to strengthen their own ability to govern themselves. For more than 200 years, the North American maroons preferred self-government in the swamps over all of the other options, and this is critical to an understanding of the Africans who arrived here and of the history of Black People in this country.

NOT TO BE

But the maroons were not the only Africans of this time period who were intent on self-government, nor were they the most numerous. By far, the largest number of Black Nationalists among the enslaved population chose to remain on the plantations, where they were watched day and night by their white captors. They worked in white people's fields, cared for white people's chattel, cooked white people's food and controlled the menial affairs in white people's homes; all in order to take advantage of the ideal time when whites could be caught off guard and slaughtered, and Blacks could be rounded up in bands that could take control of the entire area and govern it as a Black state. The overwhelming number of early Africans in America, even though they could have escaped and joined the maroons or Indian tribes, preferred to maintain contact with the white enslaver while they plotted to free themselves and grab the reins of power. These Blacks were not interested in co-existing with white people under a white controlled government; their instincts would not allow them to seriously entertain such a situation. They could feel secure only if they governed themselves, only if they possessed the power to make and enforce the laws that determined the quality of their lives; the way they had grown accustomed to doing in Africa "before the white man came."

Africans in colonial America were not fundamentally affected by the enlightened slogans and democratic philosophical opinions expressed by white people. Our forefathers heard the words and valued them, but they knew white people were incapable of practicing what they preached. And, above that, Our African-American ancestors knew that white people had one set of standards for themselves and a different set of standards for Black People. Thus, the rhetoric of the Revolutionary

War period (1760-1790) did not lead Blacks to the conclusion that the principles that necessarily implied liberty and self-government for the white colonists also implied liberty and self-government for Black People in those same colonies. Our ancestors knew that, in spite of all that was said about life, liberty and the pursuit of happiness, nothing good was intended for people of color. They therefore bided their time, watched developments, and looked for opportunities to make advances that neither the American nor British whites intended for them to make.

The same was true of the War of 1812 period. Our Ancestors participated in that war not because of promises made by the white principals, but because of the opportunities that night appear that would enable Black People to generate a result, a by-product, that neither of the warring white groups imagined probable. They were not trying to convince white people that Black People were deserving of "this" or "that"; what Black People deserved was both beyond debate and legitimate regardless of what white people thought. Our ancestors were merely looking for the opportunity to effect their objectives and live as self-governing people.

Were they delighted to hear about British abolitionist movements and declarations against the slave trade? Surely. Were they delighted to hear that the Northwest Ordinance (1787) imposed a ban on slavery in the states formed from the Northwest Territory? Certainly. Were Our ancestors delighted to hear that, as of January 1, 1808, the importation of African slaves into the United States would be prohibited? I would think so. But Our African-American ancestors were not impressed by these developments because they knew that these measures were not enacted in order to benefit Black People. Like the 3/5 Amendment, these measures were intended to benefit white people. Black People just happened to be mixed up in there somehow.

In 1800, a major revolt was planned by Gabriel Prosser and thousands of other enslaved Black Nationalists. What was their objective? The establishment of an independent Black state, a Black Nation. In 1822, Denmark Vezey, Peter Poyas and thousands of enslaved Black Nationalists plotted a major revolt. What was their objective? The establishment of an independent Black state, a Black Nation much like that of Haiti in the Caribbean. In 1831, Nat Turner and a handful of co-conspirators went on what appeared at first look to be a white bloodbath. What was it in fact? The early stages of a revolt that was aimed at establishing a Black state, a Black Nation that was governed and ruled by Black People. Scores of smaller revolts were planned during the interim years by lesser known African-Americans, all with the same objective. Thus, even at this late date, more than 200 years after the first Africans had been forced to come to America, Africans were still primarily concerned about governing themselves, enacting laws and enforcing laws that would determine the quality of Black lives. Any principle that dominates a race of enslaved yet intelligent people for that long is a principle that should never be relinquished.

ASIDES

* p. 61 ["Equality is the right to control those institutions which affect Our lives and determine Our future. It is the right to determine how Our schools are run and what is taught in them. It is the right to establish a social and economic structure that fits Our views concerning production, distribution and general welfare. It is the right to be self-determining; the right to decide if We

should pay taxes and, if so, how they should be spent. It is the right to establish a system of relationships which will be beneficial to Us, Black People. Equality has nothing to do with keeping up with whitey, individually or collectively. It has everything to do with Our natural rights, from the right to withdraw because of individual preferences to the right to join Our forces, claim land which is due Us, and establish a government which will justly represent Our cause at the conference table of nations. That is equality, Brothers and Sisters. Nothing less will do!" The People Speaks, Vol. 1, Essay 15]

The Transition Years: 1820-1860

During the colonial period, white people were pushed by two opposing forces insofar as Black People were concerned. They needed the free labor We provided in order to enjoy the standard of living they desired; but they feared that, sooner or later, Black People were going to carry out a successful revolt that would change the basic relationship between Black People and white people. Precisely because of this fear, the white leaders of this country debated the issue of abolishing the slave trade during the constitutional convention of 1787. They decided they had a few years to stretch their luck, so they resolved to not make a decision in that regard until 20 years later (1808).

What that decision would be was determined only two years later (1789) by the Black Nationalists in San Domingo, the richest colony in the world at that time. Spurred on by the desire to govern themselves and 200 years of accumulated hatred, the San Domingan Blacks drove out and slaughtered Spanish, British and French armies in succession and founded a Black Nation, which they named Haiti. News of this occurrence sent chills of horror down the backs of white Americans. As they recounted the hundreds of slave revolts that had been uncovered in the United States, there was no longer a question of whether the slave trade would be prohibited. It had to end! The question now was, "Should white people have ended the slave trade earlier? Had white people in the United States pushed their luck too far? "

White people had definitely stretched their luck, but they still had enough luck left to avoid what was due them. The revolution in San Domingo spread through the hearts and minds of Black People in the United States like a religion, and white Americans noticed the results immediately. In 1800 they dodged a bullet when the worst rain storm in memory foiled Gabriel Prosser and his 5000 Black compatriots. If it had not been for Mother Nature, the state of Virginia would have witnessed a huge bloodbath in 1800, and Black Africans would have challenged white America for control of that state.

But Mother Nature intervened; white America's luck had not run out. The importation of additional Africans into the United States in large numbers was now a definite no-no, but what was to be done with the Blacks who were here? The white leadership, as the "founding fathers" had dome in 1787, wrestled anew with this problem.

The preferred options were clearly evident, but nearly impossible to implement. The first option involved abolition, which was the code word for sending Black People somewhere else to live. The British whites had already checked into the viability of this option. In 1787, they had established the colony of Sierra Leone (in Africa) as their ideal repatriation location. By 1815, this colony had experienced survival pains and evolved into a permanent Black settlement. But was repatriation practical? After the turn of the century, there were more than a million African-Americans in the United States. The country would go bankrupt trying to repatriate even a small percentage of them. Certainly it was one of the solutions of choice, but abolition-repatriation was simply not feasible.

In addition, even though the African slave trade had been abolished, some African slaves were still being brought into the country. The economic basis of the South depended on unpaid labor, and the only persons who would work for nothing were enslaved Africans. As long as slave labor remained the mainstay of the South's economy, Africans would have to remain in this country.

Extermination of the Africans in America passed through some minds. But, the South would never allow its labor supply to be exterminated. Additionally, if it had not been for biological factors (the inability of the Native Americans to fight off white people's diseases), white people would never have succeeded in decimating the Amerindian population. Whites were able to militarily kill off only a small portion of the Amerindian population, and to attempt to do the same to better adapted and more numerous Black People would have resulted in as many white deaths as Black deaths, and could have destroyed the country that whites had fought to establish barely 20 years earlier.

If there were one thing the whites were afraid of, it was giving Black People the impression that Black People had to kill or be killed. The reports of the Spanish and French on the subject of how passionately the Blacks of San Domingo fought made a lasting impression on white Americans, and they had witnessed the same themselves, only on a smaller scale. To arouse the Black masses was not the intent of the white leaders. Their intent was to remove the Blacks before San

Domingo played itself out in the towns and cities of the United States.

The whites never considered integrating Black People into American society. Integration was the only feasible option available to whites, but that, to them, was the most horrible solution imaginable. At that time, as now, whites would have rather perish than accept Black People as equal human beings!

Thus, by 1808, repatriating the enslaved African was an impossibility, exterminating the enslaved African was an impossibility, and treating the African as a fellow American was an impossibility. White America was facing a *callejon sin salida*, an alley with no way out. White America had created a monster, a monster that they did not know what to do with. They had, in fact, created a monster that they, white people, did not have the power to control.

In 1822, a revolt involving nearly 9000 Blacks in Charleston, S. C., was betrayed by two uncle tom Negroes. Denmark Vezey, the leader of the revolt, had planned to establish a Black state wherein Black People could govern themselves. Every white person encountered, man, woman, and child, was to be killed. In 1829, <u>David Walker's Appeal</u>, which urged Black People to die in revolt rather than remain enslaved, was discovered by white people. Two years later, Nat Turner and his band of religious compatriots revolted and marched toward Black self-government. They killed whites mercilessly as they approached the seat of government, which they planned to take over and convert into a Black state. It must have seemed to the whites that doom was imminent, because African power seekers were becoming more active and more audacious than ever.

But, fortunately for the whites, they were wrong. The

Black Nationalist outbursts of the teens, twenties and early thirties did not represent an intensification of revolutionary energy among Black People. It was not proof that Black People had realized that white people were unable to control them. Instead, these Black revolts represented the last of the African Nationalists who were willing to take what was due them or die trying. Among Black People in general, a transition was taking place and making itself known. For the most part, Black People were going through changes, and the changes We were experiencing kept white people, now vulnerable white people, from suffering the consequences of their wrongs. The monster the whites had created, the monster that they had no way of controlling, was losing its instinct to kill its enemy and gallantly fight for survival.

Several factors contributed to this untimely development. It will suffice to say that, as the years passed into decades and the decades into centuries, the African population in America became less and less African and..... detached. The dominant African in America in 1830 was not the same as the African who arrived here in the 1600s. By 1830, some critical elements of Africanness had been slowly weaned out of Us. The Africans of 1830 did not value self-government like their ancestors because they had never experienced self-government. They did not know what equality was because they were uneducated, or worse, mis-educated. They did not understand what liberty implied because they had never known liberty. The metaphysical infrastructure that had made early enslaved Africans exceptional men and women was not a dominant part of the 1830s African-American. The "world" of most enslaved Blacks in 1830 consisted of white masters, work fields, ragged clothes, huts with cold dirt floors, bare feet, whippings and insults, lack of adequate nourishment, slave auctions, separated families, yearnings to be free. There was nothing healthy, nothing positive in the norm of enslaved Africans. They were not supposed to learn to read and write, and if they learned any way, what they read was white-centric news-views that left Blacks with a mostly warped picture of what was happening locally, nationally and internationally. The Africans enslaved in the 1600s wanted to be free because freedom meant self-government. The 1830s enslaved African wanted to be free because freedom meant doing whatever he or she felt like doing with his/her time. What a phenomenal drop in perspective!

The ability to adjust to extenuating circumstances had been an African strong point for thousands of years. Adapting is a proactive response; but beyond a certain limit, a firm position must be maintained. Early Africans adapted while they plotted to rid themselves of white domination. By the 1830s, however, a different reality was emerging. Instead of adapting in a proactive way, Black People had begun demonstrating a preference for "making do". They were becoming resigned to abdicating and submitting, and this at the very time when they were in a position to bring about some serious changes.

But serious changes to the early Africans meant self-government, self-determination, independence. For the Blacks of 1830, serious changes implied much less substantial objectives. In fact, "serious" might be too powerful an adjective. Simply "changes" is what Black People now wanted. The African influences (African individuals, ideas, customs, standards, etc.) had been reduced to a minimum, there was virtually no exposure to life's finer quantities, qualities nor concepts, their processes of analysis were dominated by what they saw and heard [their ancestors remembered what they had been taught in Africa— the most powerful knowledge is hidden], and they had been worn down by the constant struggle against white oppression. Self-government? Black Nationhood? These type objectives required too much energy, too much persistence, too much commitment. What Black People wanted now, more than anything else, was some relief; relief from the enervating burden of non-stop physical and psychological warfare, relief from the heavy responsibility of defending their human rights among people who blotted out their intelligence whenever the issue of race arose, relief from a steady diet of coming up short of reasonable expectations. Without consciously deciding to do so, Black People began to wave the white flag.

It was a flag that few Blacks or whites were able to acknowledge. Even historians, upon review, failed to recognize this huge historical transition. As for the principals, the whites were blind with their own assumptions, precepts and sets of probable solutions. Whites were unable to see anything Blacks did without first spicing it with their own projections. Ergo the Black Codes. Never would white people, the masters of violence, vengeance and intrigue, have imagined that Black People would let go of their own aspirations and submit to white people's terms.

As far as Blacks were concerned, this change went unacknowledged because Black People were not consciously aware of it. By all appearances, Black People continued to respond to slavery in much the same way, but the intensity and objectives had diminished. They continued to run away, but not with the maroon objective of self-government. They continued to rebel in small ways, but with short-sighted objectives. They continued to purchase themselves (when that option was available), start fires and commit acts of violence because they still wanted freedom. It's just that they no longer had an accurate vision of what freedom was. To early Africans in America, freedom without equality was slavery; to Blacks in the 1800s, freedom without equality was better than what they had become accustomed to.

As stated earlier, the lack of exposure to African ideas, ideals and concepts contributed to this loss of vision and understanding. Educational restrictions contributed immensely as well. Add the rise of the Abolitionist movement and we have all that is needed to understand why Blacks became receptive to freedom without equality.

The Abolitionist movement began in England and was active in the 1600s. Its objective was to impose a white solution to the "problem" of slavery. By the late 1700s, the Abolitionist movement had taken hold in the American colonies. By the 1830s, it was well established but had accomplished next to nothing.

However, the abolitionist propaganda had begun to infiltrate the minds of the slaves. Without doubt, during this transitional period, abolitionist propaganda impacted on Black People more than the physical presence of the Black Codes, which failed to instill fear in the freedom seekers. Not surprisingly, the key to this abolitionist impact was individuals such as Harriet Tubman and the host of slaves who were showcased by Abolitionist organizations.*

Suddenly, the Black liberation movement was dominated by underground trips to Canada, slave speeches before anti-slavery crowds, slave writings in books and abolitionist publications, Black appeals to the federal government for a Black state, court cases, migrations westward by free Blacks in search of better "treatment", repatriation advocacy and a host of other similarly oratory-oriented "activities". The Black struggle was becoming a paper struggle, a self-negating struggle, a testament to the "advantages" of self denial. The Black liberation struggle was no longer a struggle between equals, a struggle between free white men and enslaved Black men, a struggle between powerful wills. Black People had submitted, therefore We had no claim to equality; and Our "resistance" lacked the creativity and audacity of an authentic nation builder. Our struggle, the Black struggle, became a request, and remained so until white people lost control of the War Between the States.

Between 1840 and 1860, incredibly, the two most serious warriors for the rights of Black People were a Black woman and a white man. The white man was John Brown, who, even today, is the object of ridicule among white people because he tried to arm Black slaves and wage guerilla warfare against the plantation system. Everything whites say about John Brown is intended to lead one to the conclusion that he was a madman. But he was not a madman. He recognized that his race of people had committed a serious crime against humanity, and attempted to do what he could to right this wrong. If there were more John Browns among white people, a lot of suffering already would have been avoided. But whites are blind to criticisms of themselves, particularly in regard to the race issue. Because of their "blindness", their refusal to see, their unwillingness to face up to their misdeeds, and their insistence on staying the course, a lot more of unnecessary suffering is in America's future.

America has produced two historical giants. Perhaps the greatest figure of all was Toussaint L'Ouverture, the general behind the revolution in San Domingo in the early 1790s. The other, standing as tall as circumstances would allow, was Harriet Tubman.**

The United States has never produced a person as outstanding as Harriet Tubman.*** Harriet was a person of action who held true to her roots. She acknowledged no limitations to what could be accomplished, and never discounted a course of action because of purely logical analysis. Harriet Tubman had an innate understanding of that which was hidden, and as a result, possessed the vision characteristic of individuals who stand out not only from their contemporaries, but throughout the ages as well. Harriet retained much of the self-respect and psychological infrastructure that the early Africans had possessed, had an innate understanding of what liberation implied, and made the sacrifices called for in order to promote what she valued. White America will never recognize this woman (just as it will never recognize Malcolm X, Marcus Garvey or W. E. B. DuBois) because she fought against what white America stood for on her terms. But Black America might one day get off its knees, regain its dignity and give this outstanding freedom fighter her just due.

ASIDES

* p. 73 [For more on the Abolitionist Movement, see Ten Lessons: An Introduction to Black History, "The People", 1993, Lesson #5]

** p. 74 [See Ten Lessons: An Introduction to Black History, "The People", 1993, Lesson #5]

*** p. 74 [Abraham Lincoln, who had felt the sting of being discriminated against, was a distant second. The so-called founding fathers didn't have either the intelligence or the courage to end slavery, and therefore are ordinary at best.]

The Change: 1860-1876

From 1600 through the colonial period, African all the way.

From 1830 through the 1850s, evidence that changes had taken place.

The Civil War and Reconstruction and ... the emergence of the Black American mindset.

The struggle of request had begun. We couldn't make any demands; after all, We were in their country, working for them, being tolerated by them. In addition, We no longer had a group purpose that We were aware of. The best solution was to continue to request until We realized what Our next step would be.

Abolition was definitely on Black People's minds, but after abolition, what? Repatriation? Certainly, some of Us wanted to leave the United States and start over in a land where We would have better opportunities. For others of Us, repatriation was out of the question, unless, of course, the government would pay the expenses. Still others had become accustomed to the United States, had made a life for themselves here. Were they going to give up all that they had earned over the years? Not unless forced to do so. And nationhood! What about a Black country? That would be fine, but where? And under what conditions? Question after question filled the mind of Black person after Black person leading up to the 1860s, and the only elements all of them had in common were doubt, uncertainty, a feeling of helplessness. Even after the War Between the States started, these questions marked by doubt continued, because Black People knew that the Civil War was a war between white people that was not intended to benefit Black People. Regardless of which side won, the condition of Blacks, slave and free, would remain intact, unchanged.

NOT TO BE

But something unexpected happened. White people lost control of the war, and Black People took advantage of the opportunity and emancipated themselves!

Contrary to what has been popularly taught, the Emancipation Proclamation did not free the slaves, could not free the slaves and was not intended to free the slaves. As a matter of fact, the slaves had begun emancipating themselves more than a year before the Emancipation Proclamation was issued. What the Emancipation Proclamation did was legitimize the actions of these runaway slaves and open a legal alternative to abolition. The slaves, individually and sometimes collectively, thought about the possibilities presented by the war's unusual turn and decided to stop supporting the Confederate States and start supporting the North.* This change of support shifted the balance of power from the South to the North and enabled the North to emerge victoriously.

The Emancipation Proclamation made no mention of repatriation. This is the big difference between it and the abolitionist preachings. By shifting the balance of power in the War, Black slaves made freedom for Black People who had a right to stay in the United States one of their most viable options.

Black People did not ask for the 13th Amendment, which supposedly freed the slaves. We did not need to be freed because We had already freed Ourselves during the War. Black People did not ask for the 14th Amendment (citizenship) nor the 15th Amendment (the right to vote). As stated earlier, other than to gain freedom, We had not decided what We wanted to do. The same is true as regards Our role in the Reconstruction governments— We did not ask to govern the Reconstruction states. Nonetheless, these are very important events in the history of Black People in the

United States. The combined effects of the Abolitionist movement, the Emancipation Proclamation, the 13th, 14th, and 15th Amendments, and Reconstruction developments pushed Black People toward Our next step, and ever since We took that step, We have been unable to get back on the right track.

We adapted a struggle of request because We were a beaten people, a psychologically drained people. We knew We wanted freedom, but after that there was not much of a consensus on what <u>could</u> follow. <u>The important events mentioned in the preceding paragraph gave Us the impression that We could be American citizens</u>; and the whites in the North, in order to advance and realize their economic objectives, **needed** Us as citizens of the United States. The question is, "Did We, Black People, <u>need</u> to be citizens of the United States?"

Yes, United States citizenship was an option, the most realistic option We had managed to become aware of. **But it was not the only viable option We had.** According to international law, as soon as We had freed Ourselves, We had a right to decide **for Ourselves** what We wanted to do. We could even legally choose to form Our own Black government right here in America, in the states where We were most thickly populated. **We, Black People, had the right to stay where We were and form Our own government**. We had the right to govern Ourselves!! But the United States government kept this information away from Us. We were therefore cheated and defrauded, but not knowing as much, We settled for American citizenship and set out to make America the country its grand slogans, documents and laws claimed it to be.

For a small number of years after the southern and northern whites made up, Black People lived in half-fear constantly. We tried to make Ourselves invisible to the

NOT TO BE

whites who still, in spite of Our citizenship, were Our masters. Because of Jim Crow and the strategic disarming of Black People, We had to walk lightly. But this turned out to be only an intermediate posture. By the end of the Reconstruction Period (1876), more Black People had been schooled than ever before. Not only were Blacks attending secondary and elementary schools in large numbers, but colleges as well. Black People were also being more widely exposed and better able to present and defend their preferences. And, during Reconstruction, Black People had exerted the vestiges of power and begun to see grand possibilities. The struggle of request continued, but by the 1890s there was evidence that a new seed had been planted. Many of Our requests began taking on the sound of urgency, and Our struggle became marked by demands and resistance to white attacks.

Demands and resistance? Demands! Why now?

The answer lies in increased exposure and increased communication with Black People outside of the United States. We learned more and more about the strangulation of Haiti** (even in 1994 Haiti has not recovered), the degradation of Africa, the Geneva convention, the partition of Africa, forced labor in Africa and the pitiful conditions Black People in Africa were being forced to live under. Now, more than ever, We recognized Our desire to remain in the United States, a desire that was to become the defining element of the struggle of Black People in America. But, We once again began to connect Ourselves with Black People around the world, and this connection is what gave Us the courage to begin making demands. The demands were not as drastic as those of the early Africans in America, but they indicated that We were on the verge of taking the offensive. The Black movement, now less a nationalist movement and more of a humanist movement that centered around Black People, was evolving into what is now the history of the 1900s.

But let's step back for a few years. The struggle of request was still a large part of Our political program (if it can be called that), and was epitomized by Booker T. Washington. Mr. Washington, a brilliant and disciplined educator who possessed a "with all deliberate speed" mentality, preached that it was to the advantage of Black People to not compete with white people economically nor get involved in activities aimed at political or social equality for all citizens of the United States. Mr. Washington was one of the first post-Reconstruction era Blacks to ally with white people at the expense of his race. Much of what he taught was exactly what Black People needed to learn; the value of discipline, honest labor and integrity, e.g., but the context within which he wanted to apply them were totally inappropriate. He knew as much. That is why he sought all of the advantages for his family that he advised Black People in general not to seek. It would be difficult to prove that Booker T. Washington was a con man, but the game he ran had strong flim-flam overtones. His strength though, as is the case with all flim-flam operations, is that he was saying what many Black persons wanted to hear.

Not that Black People believed what Booker T. Washington was teaching. That is not why they wanted to hear what he was saying. A large number of Blacks wanted to hear what Booker Washington was saying because they were afraid of white power and wanted to avoid conflict at all cost. To such Blacks, the struggle of request was the best course to pursue. The problem, though, was that simply requesting was counter-progressive because Black People could not move forward on Our new mission— that of making America what its documents and literature passed her off as. Mr. Washington was keeping Us in the safety zone, so to speak, but more than safety was required. Something more had to be initiated.

W. E. B. DuBois presented the additional element. DuBois countered Mr. Washington's struggle of request with a struggle of demand; demand political equality, demand social equality, demand economic opportunities equal to those of whites, demand equal education opportunities, etc. Out of such a platform arose the Niagara Movement. The powers behind this movement, the powers behind the struggle of demand, were educated minds, truth, right and morality. These powers would be used to force white America to make concessions that would be beneficial to Black People in America and people of color around the world. DuBois and his followers were not prepared to inflict physical harm on white Americans; a physical confrontation, they had convinced themselves, would result in disaster for Black People. They wanted, instead, to put America's conscience and intelligence to the test, thinking that America would submit to the truth and initiate the humanity-oriented changes that were called for. They discovered that white people's conscience and intelligence, like white people's religion, recognizes limitations imposed by white people's economic and political exigencies.

Nonetheless, DuBois' struggle of demand was much more to the liking of the majority of the Black People in America. It made demands, but it wasn't confrontational; therefore, the safety zone was reasonably acceptable. When the safety line was crossed, when violence flared up between Blacks and whites, it was usually a case of white people attacking and Black

People defending. Thus, from a legal standpoint, Black People could not be honestly accused of subversion, treason or attempting to overthrow the government. It is important to note that during this time period (1890-1920), there is little to suggest that Black People in America were prone to take the offensive physically; lacking this, the concept of fighting to establish a Black Nation was far out of mind.

DuBois' struggle of demand was proving effective, insofar as the objective of making America live up to (little by little) her grand slogans and constitution was concerned. As the years progressed, circumstances of an international and national nature forced white America to concede more and more liberties, rights and privileges. White liberals, attempting to sever the independent nature of Black movements such as the Niagara movement, founded organizations such as the National Association for the Advancement of Colored People (NAACP), with the *Crisis* magazine as its propaganda organ. The *Crisis* was edited by Mr. DuBois, who was constantly criticized by the white liberals for his radical and uncompromising positions. Whites continued to support the NAACP, however (for fear of a more radical alternative emerging), and provided funds that Black People themselves were not able to invest in the struggle. It is important to remember that these liberal whites were not investing funds in the Black struggle, they were investing funds in order to control and effectively monitor the Black struggle.

But the Black struggle was learning how to become an international struggle, and this helped Black People in the United States. (Without the elements that came into play as a result of internationalization, the Black struggle of demand would have been a complete failure.) Dr. DuBois, in his desire to make sure that Black People

NOT TO BE

in Africa were able to govern themselves, helped organize several Pan-African congresses. These congresses brought Black People from the seven continents to the same table, where they discussed politics and economics and initiated plans of action that made the Black struggles throughout the world appear as one struggle. The power of this spectacle, particularly after Black controlled governments began emerging in Africa in the 1950s and 1960s, did more to advance the civil liberties of Black People in the United States than any action We took within this country's boundaries. The Africa from whence We came, the Africa that We had renounced in favor of America, the Africa that We still did not want to return to was, in her own way, looking out for her lost sons and daughters. We had deserted Mother Africa, but Mother Africa had not deserted Us.

More than 300 years had passed since Black People first stepped foot on this continent as slaves. How far We had descended since then! Our aspirations, Our perceptions, Our understanding, Our toughness physically and mentally; all were mere skeletons of what they had once been. In spite of this, here Black People were in the early 1900s participating in a struggle that would change the nature of world relations during the 20th century. To lose so much yet retain, nonetheless, enough to promote ideals that were "ahead of their time" speaks evermore to the strength and native intellect of Mother Africa. Mother Africa was arousing herself inside of Us, individually and collectively, and Her call was proving impossible to resist.

Dr. DuBois' emphasis on Pan-Africanism was one response to Mother Africa calling. Dr. DuBois, then, took Black People back to Africa ideologically, metaphysically. Right on DuBois heels was Marcus Mosiah Garvey. Garvey's calling was a physical one;

ideas were good, but being in Africa and governing Ourselves was even better.

Marcus Garvey's "Back to Africa" movement was fascinating, but it had little chance of succeeding. The factors that combatted against the repatriation efforts of the 1800s were still too great to overcome, and the inability of Black persons from the United States to colonize parts of Africa had been made clear by earlier Black entrepreneurs like Paul Cuffee and Alexander Crummell. Even the thought of Black People leaving the United States for the purpose of colonizing Black People in Africa is ludicrous. What is amazing, to the contrary, is that this ludicrous proposal re-awakened Black People in this country and started Us to seriously think again in terms of Black Nationhood.

Marcus Garvey is the epitome of his movement. Garvey was a great man, not because of his strengths but in spite of his huge weaknesses. Garvey was a capitalist, an egoist, color struck, tactless and lacking of the management skills needed to steer a major movement, yet he was able to mobilize the minds, spirits and bodies of Black People in America in a way that no Black person had been able to do since Reconstruction. Not since the Civil War had such a movement involved the active participation of the Black masses, and mass mobilization for a similar reason has not been repeated in America since Garvey. For the first time in a long time, Black People were able to relate positively to the sound of Blackness, and that is a necessary step toward actually feeling Blackness as a positive element.

Even though Garvey's movement was a back to Africa movement, there were not many Blacks who were actually willing to physically leave America for good. As was stated earlier, the former slaves wanted to be

Americans more than anything else. Their support of Garvey represented another response to the call of Mother Africa. They had wanted to hear what Booker T. Washington said because they needed to feel safe, to feel that they did not have to provoke white America's ire. Black People had wanted to hear what W. E. B. DuBois was saying because they couldn't accept total surrender— they had to be assertive in some manner. They also wanted to hear what Marcus Garvey was saying. Garvey was more popular than either Washington or DuBois, but Black People's response to him was based on what he offered that they felt they needed. Black People needed to feel good about themselves, they needed that vicarious contact with Africa and they needed to acknowledge the Africa that was inside of them, but Black People did not feel the need to return to Africa.

Thus, Garvey's movement failed to reach its stated objective. There was not enough leadership at the top, and not enough mass support at the base. Add to this the insidious interference of white governments (including that of the United States of America), and Garvey's destiny becomes easily understood.

But Garvey's movement was not a failure, not by any means. Up to this point in history (1994) it has not produced the pronounced consequences of DuBois' Pan-African initiative, but it might prove to be more beneficial in the long run. Garvey's movement started Black People in the United States to thinking about self-determination again. For the first time since the 1830s, Black People were thinking in terms that could result in Black Nationhood. The approach to Black empowerment of Garvey's followers can in no way be compared to the empowerment efforts of the maroons and slave revolutionaries, but time can make a comparison legitimate if sufficient progress is made in that regard by future generations of Blacks. Such progress would represent the final link in Our redevelopment after the transition that took place decades earlier. It offers the hope that even though Black People are still not ready to go back to Africa, We will become ready to take on the responsibility of governing Ourselves and providing for Our own well-being.

From the 1920s through the present, we have witnessed a continuation of these two paths. The overwhelmingly dominant path has been the struggle of demand, which has come to be known as the civil rights movement. This struggle, as was stated earlier, benefited more from the advances made by Pan-Africanism than it did from its own protest activities. The smaller path, the path to Black Nationhood, has been sabotaged enormously by the United States governments to the point that a huge number of Black persons still do not know of its existence. But it is there, alive and kicking, although its chances of dominating the hearts and minds of African-Americans now seems slim. We will briefly trace each of these paths. Surprises and complexities abound.

ASIDES

* p. 77 [By remaining on the plantations and doing their usual work while the War Between the States went on, the slaves were actually supporting the South. When the slaves began running away to Northern armies, the South didn't have anyone to do the work the slaves had been doing. As a result, the South's internal structure collapsed, the Confederate soldiers could not be supported and the South lost the War. See Black Reconstruction by W. E. B. DuBois]

NOT TO BE

** p. 79 [After gaining independence, the Blacks of Haiti wanted to establish normal relations with other countries. However, the white nations, including the United States, conspired to punish the Black Haitians for ending their slave condition. The white nations refused to carry on normal relations with Haiti and blockaded Haiti's ports so that no other country was able to do business with Haiti. These actions forced Haitians to turn on each other and started Haiti toward becoming the poverty stricken and dictator dominated country it is today. See <u>The Black Jacobins</u> by CLR James]

Civil Rights

The Civil Rights movement, as a Black movement, began in the 1830s, in the transitional period that was discussed earlier. It is during this period that most Blacks in the United States subconsciously decided that they didn't want to fight anymore; at least, not on terms that immediately brought out the worst in white people. Henceforward, Our ultimate human and political rights would be temporarily de-emphasized; We would not demand true equality, self-government, or anything of the sort. Black People would let white people rule and, later, restrict the Black struggle to seeking access to the rights and privileges that were due Us as constitutional citizens of the United States. Black People would seek objectives more along white people's terms than Our own. Black People would surrender, but with some minor concessions in Our favor.

The Black Civil Rights movement in America has been composed of very diverse elements. Included is the Black Abolitionist movement, elements of Black Reconstruction, the migrations west symbolized by Moses "Pap" Singleton and the Exodusters, the struggle of request associated with Booker T. Washington, the struggle of demand associated with W. E. B. DuBois, and some elements of followers of Marcus Garvey. This diversity has enabled the Civil Rights movement to attract large numbers of persons, and it is by far the dominant struggle against racism in the United States.

The Black Abolitionist movement and Reconstruction have already been mentioned in this essay and are discussed in more detail in <u>Ten Lessons: An Introduction to Black History</u> (Mbulu, The People, 1980, 1993). The Exodusters, Black People who travelled west after the Civil War in search of better treatment, were much like their maroon ancestors. The maroons, you will remember, wanted total self-government; the Exodusters, including those who migrated prior to the Civil War, were willing to settle for much less— a Black run town or county that was part of the overall United States government system, isolation from whites, or simply "better treatment" (civil rights). Hundreds of thousands of Blacks uprooted themselves, battled against the odds of survival and travelled in search of a better life. Many of these Blacks would probably have opted for total self-government if they had known they had the right to establish a Black country here (in the United States). But they did not know, so they settled for what looked like the next best thing.

The spirit of the Exodusters is present in many of the followers of Marcus Garvey. Garvey's movement advocated the physical relocation of Black People from the United States to Africa. Black People liked the spirit of this idea, but Black People were not going to leave the United States in large numbers. It is safe to say that, of the millions of persons who supported the Garvey movement, few would have been willing to actually cross the Atlantic one final time. Yet, the fact that they wanted to be beyond the power of white government is beyond doubt.

Thus, the followers of Garvey, whose rhetoric is nationalist but whose actions are clearly less than nationalist, could very well be grouped as civil rights organizations or movements. After all, substance is what defines and sustains reality (appearances are not profound enough to dictate terms). A perfect example is a Black power organization such as the Nation of Islam. The economics of the Nation is crystal clear; like Garvey, it is capitalist. The religion of the Nation is also clear; its Afro-centric version of Islam recognizes that Our race is critical to Our proper development. But what about the politics of the Nation? Has it ever actually initiated a program, an actual program, that sought independence and self-government for Black People? Surely, it speaks of nationalism in its 10 Point program entitled "What the Muslims Want." But the terms used are perplexingly solicitous and non-assertive. To wit, it speaks of Black People being "allowed to" establish a separate state, of white people having the obligation to "maintain and supply Our needs" for 25 years, of exemption from taxation, of "equal employment NOW," etc. Nationalists do not request, they demand. Their tone is one of power [sometimes simply presumed], not impotence. And, their objectives are clear. The Nation of Islam, on the other hand, wavers between requests for a separate state and employment opportunities within the status quo. The talk is Garvey, it seems; the walk, however, is DuBoisian.

But wait! Being a DuBoisian nationalist is not such a bad thing. After all, the effective back to Africa movement was spearheaded by DuBois. Through Pan-Africanism, many African Blacks were able to regain control of their governments. Meanwhile, in the United States DuBois is the Pan-Africanist who was laying the foundation for America's 20th century civil rights movement. The Niagara movement stated the intention Black People had of independently attempting to resolve the issue of racial inequality. White "liberals", fearing the power of an independent Black movement, quickly threw their money, influence and resources behind a civil rightist, white dominated organization called the National Association for the Advancement of Colored People. This organization, for all intents and purposes, swallowed the Niagara Movement and DuBois himself became editor of the *Crisis*, the propaganda news arm of the NAACP. The NAACP pushed forward because of and in spite of white liberal involvement, and some of the most easily recognized Black names emerged from its ranks.

The same can be suggested of the National Urban League, which was initially focussed around helping Black People adjust to life in the cities. As the years passed, the NAACP and the Urban League established the civil rights movement across the length and breadth of the country. Even though they spent most of their time fighting specific evils such as lynchings, judicial inequalities, Jim Crow, and thousands upon thousands of racist incidents and responses, their overall aim was social, economic and political equality for Black People. These two well-known organizations, and many others like them, marked the period between 1910 and 1950 as challenges to racial injustice and demands for effective corrective legislation. It was a period of making white America aware of her maltreatment of Black Americans, and proving to white America that Black Americans belonged. It was DuBois' struggle of demand bolstered by threats of civil unrest. Has this effort produced results? Needless to say it has. Has this effort affected the basic power relationship in the United States? I suggest not. Has this effort changed white people ideas about Black People? On the surface, yes; in reality, no. What impresses white people is the ability of someone to instill fear in their hearts and minds. Black People, since the days of the maroons, have not even attempted to produce such a response.

Needless to say, the Black men and women who spearheaded the civil rights movement in this era were brilliant. But, in the same way that racism undermines the intelligence of white people, the drive to achieve recognition from white people undermined the intelligence of many Black activists. Some of the steps many Black activists insisted on taking were absolutely void of logic and self-esteem. For example, Black leaders insisted that Black men be allowed to fight in America's wars. Thousands of whites who had received all of the benefits America had to offer refused to fight for their country, but Black leaders insisted that Black men be allowed to get shot and die for America's exploitative objectives. If they were insisting because of economic reasons (a steady income, for example), then fine; that is understandable. If they were insisting in order that Blacks gain access to and learn how to operate certain equipment, arms, machines, etc., then fine; that is understandable. But to insist that Black People be allowed to go to war for the purpose of proving to white people that Black People were willing to die for white America's objectives; that, that certainly, is absolutely ridiculous.

What happened between 1910 and 1950 in the civil rights movement repeated itself between 1950 and 1980. The fight against institutionalized injustice and discriminatory laws continued, as did the thousands upon thousands of challenges to individual acts of discrimination. The 1940s and 1950s witnessed millions upon millions of Blacks migrate to urban areas throughout the country, and these Blacks became exposed to ideas and examples that rendered them less and less satisfied with the slow corrective responses they were getting from white America. Meanwhile, the Blacks who remained in the rural areas, the south, were getting "tired of being tired" of white America's excesses. As a result, the civil rights movement moved into another gear. Black People in the north and south began to seek attention as they made demands. The attention getter the southern Black civil rights activists used was the sit-in/non-violent demonstration. The attention getter the urban Black civil rights activists used was the riot.

The attention getters carried out in the south were well-orchestrated, led by individuals and organizations with game plans that would shame white America before the world, force the federal government to support the rights of African-Americans, and destabilize the economy of the community where the demonstration or sit-in took place. While withdrawing Black support of white businesses, the demonstrations also created a climate that reduced white people's ability to carry on business as usual. The resulting economic losses and financial frustrations forced white people to either make concessions to Blacks or go bankrupt. The whites, after futilely resorting to violence in attempts to disrupt the Blacks, reluctantly began to make concessions.

The parameters that defined the riots, the attention getter used by urban Blacks, was quite different. The riots were spontaneous. There was no leadership cadre that planned a riot or spelled out its objectives. The masses, the street people, the grass roots Blacks, would take as much as they could, and when they couldn't take anymore, they would explode. Their objectives were to create chaos, loot, obtain a degree of immediate gratification, and let the authorities know. There was no

NOT TO BE

underlying motive of seizing power, establishing Black rule or forcing white America to make concessions. There was simply a huge release of energy, an attack on property, a tiring out and remission, followed by participation in a government study. Even the thought of a riot made white people's knees buckle under.

The objectives of the riots were puerile, but the affect of the riots was beyond contradiction. This is true because the riots possessed an element of psychological warfare. All of the whites in the suburbs shuddered in fear as they wondered how long it would be before the riots reached their homes and families. Additionally, the riots affected the economy of white America like a natural disaster would— it hit Americans and white businessmen in the wallet and blew a huge hole in their pockets. Though unplanned and unorchestrated, the riots had the same effect in the urban areas as the demonstrations and sit-ins had in the southern areas. In order to save themselves from financial disaster, white people had to make some concessions that would relieve the frustrations of Black America.

The riots, demonstrations, sit-ins, etc., were civil rights activities that fed on each other. But neither, individually nor collectively, produced the result that civil rights activists desired, the recognition by white people that many Black individuals are "worthy". This recognition is critical to civil rightists because their unspoken objective is to be assimilated by white America, and this assimilation process cannot be agreed to unless white America accepts the inherent worthiness of Black Americans.

But Black America is paying the price for this ill-advised and ill-fated course of action. Since the late 1960s, white America, under the guise of integration, has succeeded in using its technology to reduce the self-esteem of Black youngsters to an all-time low. White America, under the guise of integration, has succeeded in turning the Black community against itself to an extent never before experienced. As a consequence of integrationist "gains," Black youngsters have little substantial concept of who they are or what their role is as a responsible member of society. More than any other group of people, Black People need to be mature, disciplined and persistent, but integrationist objectives have rendered Us more likely to seek individualistic and immediately gratifying ends. And, worst of all, Black attention to integrationist objectives has left Black youngsters defenseless in the wake of white attacks on the metaphysical foundation of Black life. The late 1980s and early 1990s have witnessed the emergence of the killer element in Black communities throughout the country. There is now a generation of Black persons who don't care about the welfare or feelings of others, who don't expect to live to reach maturity, and who don't mind killing a fellow Black person who stands between him and what he wants, no matter how trivial what he wants might be.

This attitude characterizes Black females as well as males. There is, in reality, an invisible war taking place within the Black community. The young men and women who are at the forefront of this war are extremely intelligent, but without direction. In spite of integrationist "gains," they realize that they have been made fall persons because they have no worthwhile future to look forward to. They have fingered white people as the cause of their hopelessness. They have established white people as the enemy and have declared war on white people, but actually wage war against other Blacks in the Black communities!! Black civil rights leaders deplore the acts of violence in the Black

NOT TO BE

community and urge efforts on the part of the federal government to eliminate the hopelessness. But it is the fact that Black People have surrendered the destiny and control of the Black community to white governments ("integration")* that generated this condition in the first place. These are not isolated, indiscriminate killings that are taking place. Quite to the contrary, there is a war going on, and Black People have been programmed to kill other Blacks instead of their enemies.

The civil rights movement, the struggle of request-demand, has been embraced by more Blacks in the United States than any other movement. Unfortunately, its epitaph will not refer to the increased number of Black professionals, millionaires, justices, office holders and majority figure heads; its epitaph might very well refer to the disruption of several generations of Black lives and the destruction of the metaphysics of the Black community. Hopefully, We can still avoid that end, but if We don't, it would be a fitting result for a group of people who "cut off their nose to spite their face;" who denied their own essence in order to force less developed strangers to recognize them and accept them as "equals."

Thus, we have presented the civil rights struggle of Black People in the United States. Civil rights objectives dominated Black efforts, but there were other valiant efforts as well. We will briefly review one of these efforts, the most logical of the options, and draw a close to this essay.

ASIDES

* [What civil rightists call integration is actually the assimilating of some Black individuals and the systematic elimination of others. The civil rights leadership has lost its reason for being; it is now primarily concerned about

the advancement of <u>certain</u> colored persons; civil rightists are willing to sacrifice the mass of Blacks if that will increase their chances of reaching their individual goals.]

Self-Determination

The Black Nationalist movement in the United States almost disappeared. Beginning in the 1830s, Black People spent less and less time seeking self-determination and more and more time seeking better treatment from white people. During the Civil War, Black People took advantage of the circumstances and freed themselves, and probably would have opted for independence and self-determination if they had known that that option was available. But the United States government conspired to keep Black People from realizing that they had the right to establish a government of their own on land that they already occupied, and Black People ended up settling for American citizenship instead. Thus began, in earnest, the struggle of request and the struggle of demand.

This is not to suggest that Black People did not want to govern themselves; in the 1860s they certainly did. The point being made is that Black People had stopped taking actions that could result in them governing themselves. Between 1870 and 1900, Black People were more concerned about becoming buffalo soldiers than Black freedom fighters. They were more concerned about getting Jim Crow laws repealed than making their own laws. They were more concerned about getting a decent paying job than becoming economically self-sufficient. No, self-determination was not very much a part of Our thought patterns during the post-Reconstruction period through the turn of the 20th century.

The person who inspired Black People to think anew in terms of self-government was Marcus Mosiah Garvey.

More important than what Garvey said was the spirit in which he said it. More important than what Garvey did was the ostentatious and boisterous way that he did it. To describe Marcus Garvey's appearance, one had to go beyond physical parameters. To describe Marcus Garvey's message, one had to go beyond what he actually articulated. Marcus Garvey, the individual, was a flawed individual (like all of us). Marcus Garvey, the theoretician, was a flawed theoretician. But Marcus Garvey, the symbol of Black pride and defiance, was exactly what Black People needed.

It was Marcus Garvey the symbol that grabbed the imagination of Black People after the turn of the 20th century. Because of Garvey, We began to like what We looked like and feel proud about Our race. Because We began to feel racial and self pride again, We began to want to make the decisions that would affect the quality of Our lives. And, because We wanted to make important decisions again, We thought not in terms of being integrated-assimilated by white people, but in terms of governing Ourselves.

But Black People did not want to leave America, and Garvey did. Being intelligent and open minded, We understood Garvey and supported him with all of the time, skills and money that We could muster— short of returning to the Motherland. "Back to Africa" for Black People in America was more a Pan-African reality than a physical reality. We would re-affirm Our African roots, We would support African revolutions and drives toward self-government and democracy, and We would acknowledge, both ideologically and actually, Our unbreakable ties to the Continent; but We were not going to return there and start all over again. To Us, America was home, and self-determination was inextricably bound to the land that We had occupied, worked and sweated to develop for more than 300 years.

It is important to note that, since the United States government railroaded Marcus Garvey, there has not been one, not one, substantial back to Africa movement among Black People in this country. In contrast, Our spiritual and functional ties to the Continent have grown by leaps and bounds, and the concept of self-determination has emerged as a staple within Our thought processes. The reason the actual expression of Black nationalist sentiments has been dwarfed by civil rights activism is because of the land dilemma. How do We, Black People, take the land We have a right to possess from the most powerful country in the world? The mere thought of that question proved to be too much for the overwhelming majority of Blacks to bear.

But there were many who could bear the thought.

When Elijah Muhammad started the Nation of Islam, he knew that Black People needed to be self-governing. He knew that Black People needed a nation of their own, but he also recognized that such a task was too much for him to handle. How does one go about establishing a nation from a seed; what does that involve? It would take some powerful minds to answer such questions and lay out a game plan, but the minds in the Black community that were powerful enough to do so did not apply themselves to the task because they did not view Black Nationhood in America as an attainable alternative. Thus, for more than 25 years, Black Nationalism remained a sentiment without a program, a thought that lacked sufficient expression. And then along came Malcolm X.

The Nation of Islam provided Malcolm X with the base of operations he needed to unclog the thought processes of Black People in the United States. Malcolm's powerful and well-learned mind (he only received a small dab of America's educational pill) was able to unravel the conundrums that dumbfounded Elijah Muhammad, so Malcolm was able to develop a Black Nationalist game plan and teach it to all who wanted to learn. In order to overcome the psychological cramp that immobilized Us whenever We thought of the power of the United States, We learned that We had to think of Black Nationalism in international terms and perspectives. Immediately, We were able to see Ourselves as part of an international alliance whose combined power dwarfed that of the United States. We stopped viewing the United States as a big, bad bully, and started viewing it as an entity that had several economic, political and military weaknesses that We could turn to Our favor. Secondly, We were told that We had to start defending Ourselves against the aggressive physical assaults of white people. Malcolm urged that We form community rifle clubs to facilitate this end, because defending Ourselves was a key element to developing and maintaining self-esteem and racial pride. And, Malcolm stressed the importance of a land base to the revolutionary (self-determination) process. A land base had to be identified and focussed on; that way, Black People could present a logical and coherent case to Our international allies and to the mass of Black People who would eventually determine the success or failure of Black nationalist endeavors. Now, Our nationalist thoughts could flow freely again. Black People could imagine, Black People could be creative, Black People could set Black Nationalist wheels in motion and Black People could take Malcolm's ideas to higher levels of precision and development.

Malcolm X's teachings served as the basis for the development of the Black Panther Party. Though the Panthers frequently spoke in terms of revolution,

revolution to them was a Black nationalist objective. The Panthers stressed self-sufficiency, internationalization and arming for self-defense purposes. Because the Panthers were advocating a course of action that could change the power relationship between Blacks and whites in the Americas, they were illegally and cowardly "set-up" and ambushed at every opportunity by forces of the United States (state and federal) government. Black Panther Party leaders were assassinated by government leaders, and the organization itself was sadistically gutted by representatives of the law and the United States judicial system. But the damage (from the whites' point of view) had already been done. The idea of Black Nationalism had been radically re-introduced to the masses of Black People. Black People still didn't quite understand it all, but something about the pig-like reaction of the United States authorities to the Black Panther Party generated a gut reaction that the Panthers were on to something real.

But the Panthers did not pose nearly the threat that the Republic of New Afrika posed. Although more popular and better known than the RNA (Republic of New Afrika), the Panthers did not have the time to speak in the clear Black Nationalists terms that the leaders of the RNA used, so the RNA was able to bring the message of Black Nationalism and self-determination to the Black masses in a way that could not be misunderstood. In addition, the Republic of New Afrika expanded on Malcolm's concept of internationalization and produced legal briefs and historical facts that justified more clearly the right of Black People to self-government. These briefs were presented to the United Nations. The Republic of New Afrika also identified five adjoining states in the southern part of the United States that Black Americans had a legal claim to, and organized

NOT TO BE

missions into those states to educate the Black population and arrange for a plebiscite (a vote) whereby the Blacks could decide if they wanted self-government or not. The RNA also organized a militia for self-defense purposes, and envisioned organizing a Nationalist Army that could take offensive measures if and when such proved necessary. Like the Panthers, the RNA was illegally attacked and decimated by the forces of the United States federal and state governments.

Moving into the 1980s, it seemed that the forces of Black Nationalism had once again been forsaken by the Black masses. As in the 1860s, the Black masses had been grossly misinformed and undermined by United States government forces. The U. S. government, with the help of Negro leaders/lackeys, painted negative pictures of Black Nationalist organizations and the Black Nationalist concept, and the masses, like the masses generally do, did not check into the matter and discover the truth for themselves. This powerful propaganda campaign proved very effective, so much so that not only whites, but many Blacks as well, felt relieved when Black Nationalist leaders were jailed and assassinated and organizations were destroyed.

But there were also many internal contradictions that militated against the success of a Black Nationalist movement in this country. To begin with, the idea of Black Nationalism was never adequately presented to the Black masses. Civil rights activists were on television, radio, in the newspapers and magazines, in the schools and churches, and everywhere else. Black nationalist activists, by contrast, forced no such positive exposure. As a result, Black Nationalism has failed to become a part of the consciousness of African-Americans. Secondly, the Black Nationalist movement in the United States has been composed of a disproportionately high percentage of theoreticians. These theoreticians are very useful during planning stages, but beyond that they have been unable to effectively double as Black Nationalist operatives/operators. This explains why Black Nationalist functions seem to be characterized by lack of organization, waste and inefficiency. Thirdly, most Black nationalists are "on the rebound"; if they had been treated "fairly" by America, thoughts of self-government would never have entered their minds. Even so, they straddle the fence, reluctant to "let the American dream go," but also reluctant to totally forsake Black Nationalism. And, the Black Nationalist movement has failed to make effective use of the element of violence. Black People have traditionally thought of life in sacred terms. Even though We recognize that white people have been Our mortal enemy for thousands of years, We have been unable to de-humanize them. We continue to see them, and all other peoples, as human beings with human rights who possess the sacred gift of life bestowed upon them by Mother Nature.

As we approach the year 2000 CE, the Black Nationalist movement, though weak, could receive a powerful shot in the arm. If this shot can somehow be brought to pass, the old maroon mentality will re-introduce itself to the Black struggle, and visions of thousands of Nat Turners could settle within the collective psyche of "America." The conclusion to this essay will amplify this possibility.

NOT TO BE

Conclusion

For the most part, Black People in the United States, African-Americans, have decided that they want to integrate and melt into America's pot rather than separate and make the crucial decisions that will determine the quality of life for Black males and females. History seems to be quite clear on this point. But history also seems to be quite clear on a second point— that integration is more harmful to Black People than beneficial. While Black People devise and initiate plans to integrate, white people make subliminal use of today's technology to destroy Our essence. History suggests, then, that the ultimate consequences of Our integrationist initiatives will be either the physical or spiritual elimination of African-Americans.

Physical elimination? No way! That is out of the question. Spiritual elimination? What an ominous threat! How dastardly!!! A more slimy approach to genocide is hardly imaginable. But slime flourishes in the white gestalt, the white "environment." Is a dark skinned person with a "white" mind an African/African-American? If such dark skinned persons came to dominate the economic, social and political processes of the United States, or shared equality within them, would Black People have succeeded in integrating with white people? Would civil rights then be a reality, or would white people have succeeded in destroying the essence of Blackness, in maintaining the status quo, in ensuring that power remain in the "right" hands, and in sustaining the "white way" of life? If the latter be the case, then Black People must ask if the principles of integration have been too cosmetic to effectively combat forces as profound as racism and white supremacy. Right now, none of Us seem to know, but the closer We get to the wall, the clearer the writing is becoming.

White America has virtually destroyed the Black Nationalist movement, and it has made a comical prostitute of the civil rights movement. Civil rightists are confronting a mirage; they are confronting the image of white supremacy, while white supremacy itself marches on undeterred while waging a profound war against the essence of Black People. Black Nationalists are not combatting the image the civil rightists have been suckered into confronting. Black Nationalists are fighting the essence of racism, white supremacy and human degradation. This is, in fact, the grand struggle.

However, the Black Nationalist movement needs to be imaginative, creative and audacious, particularly if it is to impact at all on African-Americans. Unfortunately, the present cadres of Black Nationalists do not exhibit those essential qualities. Where, then, lies the salvation of Black Nationalism in the United States of America?

While the civil rights movement and integration have dominated the aspirations of African-Americans, white America has subtly used its technology to destroy the metaphysical foundation of several generations of Black youth. In 1994, these young Black men and women are crowding street corners and showcasing their lack of development at every available opportunity. As was stated earlier, these young people, we'll call them "ganstas," are extremely intelligent. They are convinced that the future holds nothing good for them, and they have identified white people as the architects of their hopelessness. Do these young people have imagination? Without a doubt. Are these young people creative? Without a doubt. And, are these young people audacious? Certainly, more audacious than anything else. But, moreover, these young people have a capacity to destroy life, to injure and kill, that has been missing in previous generations of African-Americans. If these "ganstas" ever begin to educate themselves and develop some political discipline, if they ever start learning how to concentrate their anger against those whom they identify as the enemy, and if present-day Black Nationalists can devise a method whereby we can establish contact with these youngsters, politicize them and expose them to the concepts of social and racial responsibleness, then, then, Black Nationalism will impact on African-Americans and white Americans to no end. These young people already know that civil rights is a farce, that they have been betrayed by it. Something that deals with the reality of their existence and their legitimate right to respond and survive could turn them on and get all Black People to working towards more logical solutions to Our woes.

A whiff of something special lingers longer than a nose full of something ordinary. We shall see what time reveals.

Also Available From
"The People"

Spotlight on
MALE
FEMALE
Relations

ISBN 1-883885-00-0
$4.00

ISBN 1-883885-10-8
$8.00

BLACK
SMART

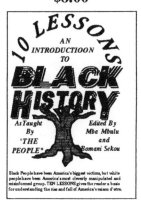

ISBN 1-883885-09-4
$10.00

ISBN 1-883885-06-X
$12.00

Send Money Order to:
"The People"   P. O. Box 50334
Washington, D. C. 20091-0334